MOON BLUE

By

Roy Irwin Gift

Moon Blue
Copyright © 2011 by Roy Irwin Gift
ISBN 978-0-9834956-1-1
Library of Congress Control Number 2011930889

SpiritBooks
wilson@spiritbooks.me

For more information: www.spiritbooks.me

**1.World War II 2. Segregation Era 3. Post-Traumatic Stress 3.Murder Mystery
4. Inter-racial Relations 4. History, Raleigh, North Carolina**

Permission granted by Stackpole Books to quote from *Combat Leader's Field Guide*, Twelfth Edition Copyright © 2000 by Brett A. Stoneberger

Printed in the United States of America by Lightning Source

Cover design by Tamaris Johnson
First Edition 2011

Acknowledgements

This book is dedicated to John and Kim Brewer of Tucson, Arizona, who listened with amazing grace as I read stories to them that evolved into this novel.

I would like to thank Chris Tucker, a genius at story-telling, who helped with ideas, suggestions, and an endless stream of questions.

Julie Simpson and Cassie Koslen must be thanked for their copy-editing and helpful criticisms. I am grateful to Walton Joyner of Raleigh, who marked up a proof with suggestions, which I heeded, and notes on Raleigh history, where he caught a few slips of my memory. I would also like to thank Barbara Rogers, whose experience as a professional writer enabled her to edit the text into a finished work of fiction.

The stories about Guadalcanal were told to me by my brother, Daniel Wolfe Gift, who survived three major campaigns of World War II. He was not awarded a Medal of Honor, but he and all his comrades on Guadalcanal earned that degree of recognition for their dedication and bravery under the most extreme conditions.

There are a few incidents of racist language to be found in these pages and, while these are offensive, they are a necessary part of an attempt to give a faithful representation—on a small scale—of segregation in wartime conditions during the 1940's. Holly Rollins, the principal character of this story, though he is becoming aware of and reacting to racism directed toward African-Americans, does not see the racism toward the Japanese. This is not inconsistency on his part; it is just a sign of the times.

Most of the action in this work of fiction takes place in 1943, a time in America when hatred of the Japanese was widespread and intense. During a newsreel, for example, a Japanese soldier being set ablaze by a flamethrower and shown as a ball of fire running in front of the camera, brought laughter and applause from an audience. Such anti-Japanese feelings were too high to allow a public awareness of racism at that time.

Table of Contents

Prologue

February 1943
Raleigh, North Carolina.

A loud knock on the door startled and awakened the woman. Her sense of having overslept, along with the daylight filtering through the stone walls and the silence of her alarm clock, told her she was going to be late to work again. Her boss, Herr Schwab, a man who had recently escaped the Nazis in Austria, had only one rule, which he often repeated in his heavy accent, "Doh nut late be to verk coming, pleez."

Others at the bakery accepted his rule, referring to him with affection as Herr Donuts. She was the only rebel and, though she frequently came in late, he had not reacted, not even to question her excuses—so far. On that note, she forced herself from the warm bed onto the sandy dirt floor with a new feeling of urgency.

She looked into a bucket dangling from a railroad spike and saw clear water, the reddish-brown silt of the creek having settled to the bottom overnight. As she rinsed her face, stinging pain reminded her of the injury to its left side. She examined the cut in a mirror nailed to the center post and put iodine on it. A cologne flask next to the iodine caught her eye and she took a sip from it, toasting her mirror image with the bottle and enjoying the burn of alcohol. She took a few more sips while considering whether to tell Herr Donuts she was delayed due to a fall getting off the bus. Her cut and swollen cheek were convincing enough to make it work.

Her nightgown swept the sand as she gathered her clothes and put them on, a plaid skirt and faded blouse. She headed for the door fastening her coat, though she still felt the pull of something she had not yet done. She stopped short as she remembered a long-distance call she was determined to make that morning. Woolworth's Five and Dime was on her way to work and she decided to use their telephone service. She grabbed her purse.

As she was leaving the cabin, she felt a jolt of fear at finding someone standing there. For an instant, in the soft light of daybreak, she thought it was the man who had punched her in the face. But then, by his shoulder-length hair and shabby clothes, she knew it to be her neighbor, a man whose brain was being consumed by congenital syphilis. That it was indeed Doll Baby was confirmed when she saw the baby carriage right behind him.

Breathless, she gasped, "You scared hell outta me. How long have you been here?"

The man stood before her, his face contorted, eyes closed, lips quivering like someone locked in a stammer, and his arms flapping in frustration.

She assumed he had come to visit with her and said, "I've no time to make coffee this morning. I'm late for work."

Even as she said these words, she was walking around him, headed for the creek. Having crossed over the moss-covered rocks with slow and careful steps, she started on a trail leading from the creek through the stunted trees and thick brush up to the Seaboard railroad tracks. Unseen crows screeched warnings and protests as they retreated before her. Five minutes later, she emerged from shadows onto a path parallel to the tracks heading south toward Raleigh. It was a bright and clear morning, but a soft wind coming down the right-of-way still carried the chill of a winter night.

She walked along with her head down, making sure of her footing on the narrow, rough path. When she did look up, she was startled yet again to see a man approaching her from the opposite direction. She thought it might be the track inspector but couldn't really tell because he too was walking with his head down.

She waited while he continued to walk toward her without looking up. As he was closing in on her, she recognized him and said in a harsh voice, "Coming to see me?"

The man stopped with the surprise of someone who had been lost in thought and, then, hurried forward until he was almost in her face.

"Yeah, I been gnawing all night on this and can't believe you'd make that call."

Her body stiffened and her face hardened. "I'm gonna do that at Woolies' Five Cent Store cause you ain't worth no more'n a nickel. Get outta my way."

The man was blocking the path and, even as she finished speaking, she put her left hand onto his chest and shoved him to the side. When her hand touched him, his eyes bulged. His face and neck went dark red. As she walked past, he struck over her arm, hitting her in the temple with his right fist, knocking her to the ground.

Next to her unconscious body was a flat iron bar about two feet long, half-buried in the loam. The man went to his knees beside her, snatched up the bar and struck her head with all his might. Though the first blow killed her, he continued in his rage to strike again and again.

§

About thirty minutes later, Doll Baby came out of the trees pushing his carriage. He turned toward Raleigh and moved along, paced by the soft creak-creak of the wheels and the crunch of its tires in the sandy-loam soil, music to his ears.

He didn't notice the woman until he came up to where she lay by the path. When he saw the body, he stopped and stood staring at the young black woman without blinking until his eyes were so dry he had to close them and keep them closed for several minutes. Then, he walked around the body and picked up the woman's purse. After stowing the purse in his baby carriage, he resumed pushing the carriage along the path, listening to its music once more.

When he returned home that evening and went through the objects gathered that day, he found the purse and added it to his collection, after dumping its few contents onto a heap of trash used to feed his fire. By the following morning he had forgotten about it.

Chapter One

Direct every military operation toward a clearly defined, decisive, and attainable objective.

----Combat Leader's Field Guide

Monday   March 1, 1943

The smoke and hissing steam of the train as it huffed to a stop at the Seaboard Railway station soon cleared enough for me to see down the platform. Everyone was moving toward the exit except a few porters who were going to the baggage car. I stepped onto the platform and shouldered my duffel, still on the alert for anyone trying to find me.

I went through the station and came out onto the sidewalk just as a police car slid up to the curb. A police officer jumped out before it had come to a full stop.

Pausing before me, the officer said, "Sergeant Holly Rollins?"

"In the station a moment ago," I answered. "Is the man wanted, officer?"

He said over his shoulder as he charged into the station, "Yeah! The Mayor wants Rollins to come to dinner."

I trudged off in the direction of city center.

Sure, in Washington there were messages at the Pentagon and at my hotel saying the Mayor of Raleigh wanted me to call his office. I didn't choose to do it. I was on my way to help a friend and, since Raleigh was my home town, I could remove the uniform and put on my civvies. I didn't have to salute anyone or talk to them if I didn't want to.

As to seeing people, I was surprised there was nobody I knew at the station or on the street. Though many of my friends were certain to be away in the service, there should still have been at least one person I recognized. If I continued in the direction I was going to Salisbury Street, I would find a beauty parlor opened while I was away overseas by someone who was once more than a friend to me.

Ida Patini was her name, a woman who came to the South and found her heart-home, while keeping enough of a New York edge to succeed in business. A few minutes later, I came to her address in a block of single-storied, dull-red brick buildings and saw a sign over the entrance that read:

Ida's Parlor
Purified and Born-again Beauty
The Patini Way

She once told me there were mystical and physical treatments that could restore a person to their original health and beauty. Such talk may sound foolish to some, but when your only relief is a quart of white lightning, it sounds like a voice of hope. I told her she could call it The Church of the Holy Perm. But she said that was a sacrilege.

The first time I saw Ida was just after I had been laid off during the Great Depression and had just dumb-lucked into a job at the soda fountain in the Nash Hotel. The owner gave me fifteen minutes of training and then left. The first order I got was from a young woman who told me she worked in the beauty parlor. Five minutes it took to make her soda and three more to ring up the ten cents it cost. She let me know how she was from New York where a soda was ready in a minute. Plus, she told me, Einstein said time was relative, which meant that one minute New York time was equal to ten minutes Raleigh time, maybe fifteen. She kept on and on until I finally realized she was teasing me.

"I could have done it quicker," I told her, "but with you such a good talker, I couldn't concentrate on the soda." It sounded sarcastic and stopped her cold.

On the train I hadn't let myself think what I would do if I found myself here, and now here I was. But I knew I wouldn't knock on her door. She was a part of my life before the war and had no place in my life now. I continued on my walk.

Arriving at Capitol Square, I saw stately trees shading a lawn with marble statues here and there. Two water fountains right next to the Capitol building had signs posted, reading *White Only* and *Colored Only*. Having grown up in Raleigh I was familiar with these signs. Even so, I was surprised to see them still here while we were fighting an all-out war to preserve freedom.

As I continued through the Square, I saw memorials to past wars and decided it was a good time to celebrate coming home alive instead of in a pine box. I came to a gray plaque dedicated to Old Pete Longstreet who led a North Carolina Brigade at the first battle of Manassas. Could I say a prayer of gratitude to this man, one of Lee's Generals, yet a man with the common touch? For some reason, I didn't feel ready to pray. All I came up with was a question: "How were you able to forgive yourself for all the blood?"

I sat down on a bench to work it out. I did want to be grateful for coming back, unlike my friend Powell, who was buried in a swamp on Guadalcanal. Maybe I hadn't been home long enough yet. I felt like I was still there with Powell and unable to take an interest in this tour of main street, USA. The only option that felt right to me was to get on with what I had agreed to do and then go back to active duty.

A neighbor had gotten me going on this mission, a man named Price, who lived across the street from the time I was in high school. Price read in the newspaper that I was going to be at the Pentagon to receive a medal and telephoned me there.

He started out by apologizing for calling to deliver a message from a Negro. Then, as soon as I told him that was okay, he went the other way and reminded me how he was the only one who accepted LaBelle Blue as a neighbor. We were, he said, fellow outcasts in the neighborhood, he because of the feud over the reek of his fish truck, and she as the only Negro there.

At this point, I interrupted him to explain that as the medal ceremony was coming up in less than twenty-four hours, and I didn't want to miss it, would he just give me the message, please.

Here is what he told me.

In the early dark of a cold morning, while the neighborhood was asleep and he was warming up his diesel engine, LaBelle had come out to his truck to talk to him about Lana Blue, her granddaughter. Some person or persons had assaulted Lana and beaten her to death. The police investigation, which wasn't much to start with, was brought to a halt when the Army refused to let the police talk to a paratrooper stationed at Fort Bragg. LaBelle thought that as a military man, I could talk to his commander to find out what was going on.

7

I told Price to tell LaBelle I'd come to see her soon. Then, after hanging up the telephone, I began to doubt my ability to do very much for her. I was recovering from five months in the swamps of Guadalcanal, and that battle was still surging through my nervous system. I had malaria in my blood stream and fungus clogging up my lungs. But now, here I was in Raleigh, and it was time to find out from her exactly what she wanted me to do.

As I strolled across town, I enjoyed the fresh air smelling of grass and flowers and of wet tar. There must have been a rain shower that morning, before I got in. I soon came to a neighborhood boundary, a stable housing horses used to pull milk wagons.

I turned onto Fontaine Street, which took its name from a General of Napoleon's Grande Armée who built a farm here. All that was left of it in this location were two houses and a cultivated field of crops on the north side of the street. In the era of the farm, these houses were slave quarters. The rest of the block on that side of the street was given over to wild bamboo, with Pigeon Creek running through it.

I was born in the house with dull yellow paint, the larger of the two, surrounded by bare soil with clay enough to be bright red. The two magnolia trees shading the front porch had large roots running on the surface of the clay, dividing into smaller and smaller branches and reaching every corner of the front yard. Unpleasant memories made me uneasy to be here, even though my family had moved away before the war.

The other house was of unpainted, blackened and warped planks. At present, only the top of the house and its tar roof could be seen from the street. Its deep yard, going all the way back to the creek, was a display of more than one hundred white sheets drying in the sun, hanging from clothes lines that ran in a star pattern from the house to the edges of the property. These were strung high and propped up here and there with poles to accommodate both the length and the weight of wet sheets.

The laundry business belonged to a woman who was born in this very house when it was a part of the farm. Though the farm was long gone, some of the General's French culture was still around. That's why even now this woman, LaBelle Blue, was known to her neighbors by the French word *Tante*, meaning aunt. They called her Tante LaBelle, and I used the more familiar *Tatie*.

After the farm was gone, a white-only neighborhood had pushed through here, by-passing LaBelle's block and moving the city limits out by several miles beyond it.

Her house was now separated from my former home by a six-foot, unpainted wooden fence that I had never seen before and didn't like. Was the owner using it to block out LaBelle? My parents had tried a similar stunt when they planted a hedge along that same property line and, although it grew as high, it was too skimpy to be the wall this fence was.

Standing there in front of her house, I wondered if it was worth a try to find Price who rented one of the houses across the street. I had a feeling he was at home only when his truck was stinking up the neighborhood, and it wasn't there now.

A sensation rippled over my skin that was similar to those I had sitting on a bulldozer on Henderson Field, knowing that Japanese snipers in palm trees were picking targets. I was being watched or, maybe even more than that, being appraised. Quickly, I looked around, getting an impression that the curtains of every house in sight were drawn aside.

I went down into LaBelle's yard and through the sheets to her front door. Having no answer to my knock, I went around to the back of the house and up the steps.

The open porch was about ten feet across and five feet deep, enclosed by a wide, wooden rail. A barrel of hot water stood next to the back door. Two wooden tubs sat on the rail, each with its wash board on one side and cake of lye soap on the other.

I knocked on the door, shouting, "Tatie, it's Moon." I knocked again.

The door opened, and there she stood in a pale blue dress hanging loose without a belt on her thin, strong frame. Her skin was tight and almost entirely without wrinkles in spite of her age. She had high cheek bones and a large hooked nose. Her black eyes seemed to look through me to a space a foot behind my head. Her perfect teeth were brown from the snuff packed down against her gums, pushing out her lower lip.

"I'm not deaf," she said, "just slow. Come in here."

She stepped aside to let me pass into her kitchen. As I came in, I could see everything was exactly the same as I last saw it. There was a table just large enough for two people to share a meal. There were four shelves with a few stacked dishes along the far wall. There was a potbellied stove and, in back of this, a door to the only other room in the house, her bedroom. Through the door could be seen a single bed, a table with four shoe boxes and a small pile of clothes. Driven into the far wall were a few ten-penny nails with clothes hanging from them.

She went to the stove, took a handle from a shelf behind it, lifted a stove plate and spat snuff-juice into the flames. There was a hiss when her spit hit the fire.

I moved back to the open door and stood there. The room was small and dominated by the hot stove. It seemed too warm for my damaged lungs.

She approached, looked me over carefully and said, "You don't hardly even look like the same man."

"The best part of me got left back there, Tatie, on that island."

I put my head on her shoulder.

"Welcome home, Merry Sunshine," she said.

"I thought often about you, memories to hold on to."

As I said this, I looked at her and wasn't surprised to see her treating this reunion with a stern absence of expression on her face. LaBelle had always rejected displays of sentiment.

Once I heard someone ask her about this and she said, "God gave me feelings so I can tend to my business, not to amuse you." She said it firmly, not a rebuff, just saying how it was.

She hugged me and then pushed me back and looked into my eyes, "You going back to war?"

"Not now. Not until I get better."

"How long's it gonna last?"

"Ten years, maybe. But Guadalcanal's a beginning."

In a soft voice she said, "I only want to hear about you. I don't want to have terrible pictures in my head."

This was good news. Some of the people I met in Washington wanted to know what it was like. I couldn't grasp it myself. How could I describe it to them? And my mind shied away from it anyway.

"Why don't you know when you go back?"

"I'm here on a medical furlough. The medicos keep track of how I'm doing. I'll get orders sending me back when they clear me to return to duty."

I sat down at the table, and LaBelle sat down across from me.

"Were you wounded?"

"I was nicked a few times, nothing serious. Now I have malaria and a lung fungus. The malaria is tough because you never know when it will leave. As you can see, I lost a lot of weight."

"Just a mess of skin and bones." After a pause she asked, "What's it like on that island?"

"The people are great and helped us a lot. They're Polo-Nesians, something like that. Until you get to know these people, you never met anybody one-hundred percent honest."

"Coloreds?"

"Some are dark and some about the same as Hawaiians."

LaBelle asked, "What kind of honest are you talking about?"

"They tell the truth and don't steal. A wallet full of money in the middle of a road, nobody would bother it. But, it's funny, they don't seem to know anything about property. They grow crops. In fact, along with fish that's all they've got. But they don't own farms. They just have a spot picked. Anytime they want, they can up and move to another spot."

"Why isn't that spot their property?"

"It's just not the way they think. Then, there's work. I spent a week trying to explain work to my friend Bolo who never got it."

"You have to work to raise crops."

"Everything is too easy to count that way," I explained. "One or two hours a week, they have crops in no time. An hour on the ocean and all the fish their family can eat. They sit around and talk forever."

"Moon, what if you picked a spot when you go back out there."

I considered that idea for a moment, "Well, I'd have to ask the head man, but I think I could."

"Go back and pick a spot for me to sit all day and talk, drinking café au lait."

I had never seen LaBelle in a dreamy mood before. I don't think she could imagine their life any more than they could imagine hers.

Meanwhile, the fire in the potbellied stove warmed its bottom to a red glow. Sitting as close to it as I was, I over-heated until I felt clammy and light-headed. My island fungus thought it was back home. I coughed a few times and it took hold. I began to cough and gag, as though my diaphragm was going into spasms, to a point where I could hardly breathe at all.

LaBelle took my arm and led me out onto the back porch. She turned on the faucet and pushed my head under a stream of cold water. That cooled me off. I got my breath and took one of my pills. After awhile I stopped coughing.

"I'm sorry, Moon, I should have thought about the heat. Let's go in the front and sit on the porch."

We walked around the house in silence. We were on the side away from the fence, with a view down the block and toward Pigeon Creek at the back of the yard. The farm on that side had the shredded remains of a corn crop that had been harvested months before. Bare stalks still stood in the field.

We sat down on the plank steps.

"I want to talk about Lana," said LaBelle. "Of all my family I've run off, she's the one I miss the most, and she's not coming back."

She sat there in silence, leaning on her left arm, her hand resting on a step, and gently massaging the back of that arm with her other hand. I had to wait a while before she spoke again.

"Did Mister Price tell you what happened?"

"Yes."

"Remember when Lana lived here with me? You know the worse thing she did, so bad it used to make me mad enough to swallow my snuff?"

I shook my head.

"She used to come home in a car, before the war when there was some gas, with an older man. They'd sit, late at night, in front of the house, right about there." She pointed at the street.

"She was going too far with him, was that it?"

"No, Moon, that wasn't it," she snapped. "It was the radio. They played the radio and woke up the whole neighborhood. Do you know what my situation is, living in this neighborhood? I wouldn't have all that fuss. But she never stopped doing it."

I didn't know what to say.

After a minute of silence, she continued, "Seems like nothing, now."

LaBelle was quiet for several minutes, no longer rubbing her arm, sitting quite still. I thought she was ready to bawl. Instead, she asked: "Do you know what I want you to do?"

"Not for sure. I just heard about Lana, and something about the army."

"What did you hear?"

"She was beaten to death next to the railroad tracks, near Slippery Rock Creek."

"And now, I need you and Lana needs you."

"What do you mean Lana needs me?"

"Find her killer. You're the one, Moon. We got nobody else."

"I came here to help you. Right now, that's the most important thing in the world to me. But I wasn't sent home healthy. They sent me here to recover because they needed my bed for the wounded. We need someone healthy to get out and work for you."

"You're the only one, Moon."

"How can you be so sure of that? I don't know anything about detecting or even about what was going on here when all this happened."

"I lost her, Moon. That's what was going on. A year before she got murdered. I gave up on her, and she sank out of sight. To this day I don't know what happened? I don't even know where her body is."

"What do the police say?"

"They don't say nothing. They think it was a paratrooper from Fort Bragg. That's something you can do. Go find out about him."

"You mean you want me to talk to the police to find out what they know about this man. Do they want to arrest him for the murder?"

"No, the police won't do nothing."

"Because he's a white soldier, is that it?"

"No, that's not it. My son Mose has a store over to South Street, with a comfort room out back that serves alcohol in the evenings. He told the police that Boyd was there and met Lana. The police asked Fort Bragg to send him down to Raleigh to be questioned, and they refused to do it."

"Do you think Boyd murdered Lana?" I asked. "Is he being protected?"

"All I know is that Mose told me Lana used to see him. She called him *Hoppy* because he has the same name as Hopalong Cassidy, and she likes the motion pictures."

"So, you want….." I still hadn't quite got the idea.

"Mister Price said you have some kind of award. Tell me, what's that worth, what they gave you?"

"If you mean what it would be worth at a pawn shop, I'd say fifty bucks maybe."

"No, what's it worth at Fort Bragg? Would it help you to get to see Boyd? To find out if he knows what happened. Maybe he knows who killed Lana."

For the first time, I realized that I was the right person to help her. Someone did need to find a back door into Fort Bragg, and there really was no one else around in a position to do that.

"All right, Tatie," I said. "I'll go to Fort Bragg. I'm not promising anything. Can't tell what I'll find out."

With that, we had come to an understanding, not exactly a tactical plan, but something I could do. I went inside to get my duffel and came back onto the front porch ready to go.

LaBelle took my face in both her hands. "Moon, Tell me how you are."

"What?"

"Tell me how you are." she repeated, and this time it sounded like a command.

For just a moment, I felt angry that she was ordering me around. I wanted to tell her that I had given myself up for dead and couldn't come back to life. I could add, even, that I wasn't sure I wanted to. I felt as though tears had begun to rise from my chest and stopped before they reached my eyes.

LaBelle was holding my face still between her two hands. She pulled my head forward and planted a big kiss in the middle of my forehead.

She said, "Tell me you're going to be all right."

My anger left me as I said, "I'm going to be all right, Tatie, and I wish I could say more."

But my voice rang false to my ear, and my face was hot and moist from the tears trapped behind it.

"But that's what I wanted to hear you say, Moon." LaBelle looked into my eyes. "I know you're going to be all right. I wanted to hear you say so."

There was nothing more to be said. I left her on the porch and went around behind the house, past the privy camouflaged under a shroud of ivy, to the back of the yard. I sat down on the bank of the creek by a path leading into a small wilderness of bamboo. This had been my own private playground when I was a child. Sitting here, I felt comfortable and at home.

I was beginning to calm down and to think through what had happened since I had been in Raleigh. I remembered what Ida said when I left for the war. "Do you remember how I used to come every morning to get change from you at the soda fountain?"

It was true. She used to come asking me to change a twenty. Then one day she said, "*Red Sails in the Sunset* is playing on Sunday. Let's match nickels to see who takes the other one to the picture show."

I was right stunned but got over it in a Raleigh minute and said, "All right."

She won and said to me, "I'll pick you up at seven," and left.

I had stood there hoping no customer would show up asking for a banana split. I would probably have split a pineapple instead. But remembering the past wasn't going to help me now, and I needed to focus on LaBelle Blue.

The cellar door of my old house got my attention and I remembered how my father and I had practically rebuilt the place, including digging a three-room cellar out of the rock-hard clay underneath.

Among my earliest memories from the time I lived there is the first time I met LaBelle Blue. I knew of her already as an aunt since everyone in my family referred to her as Aunt LaBelle, the same way they addressed all my other aunts. Both my parents had lots of brothers and sisters and, since all were married, I had quite a few aunts. But, then came an event that confirmed LaBelle as my auntie, my Tatie.

One day when I was five years old, I stumbled on one of the cracks in the sidewalk and fell down on a plank. Two rusty nails went right through the palm of my hand and stuck out the back. Though I can no longer remember being afraid or in pain, I do still remember not knowing what to do with my hand nailed to a plank because that was a new situation for me.

The best idea I came up with was to go see Aunt LaBelle who was nearby hanging up sheets in her yard. I raised myself up and, hugging the long plank to my chest and dragging it, walked sideways-backwards down the stairs to where she was working.

She may have been surprised to see me backing up to her with a plank nailed to my hand but didn't make any fuss. She gently took hold of the plank and my hand and pulled it free in one steady and continuous motion. She picked me up and carried me through her house to a tub on the back porch, where she held my hand under a faucet until the bleeding stopped. She washed the wounds with soapy water.

Using a small handkerchief she took from the pocket of her apron, she bandaged my hand, making a knot that fit into my palm. Sitting there at the table on her lap, I ate the cookies and milk she gave me and enjoyed her hugs and kisses. My mother was dead and my new stepmother didn't like me. I could hardly remember a time when someone had been so good to me.

I looked at the back of my right hand. There were two tiny spots where the nails had come through. I stared at those spots and this time tears did come into my eyes. As I sat on this familiar creek bank, they began to drip from my face onto my shirt and pants. I thought of Lana and of those who died on Guadalcanal, those I knew who died and others I didn't know, including the Japanese. LaBelle was right. I was going to get better, but I wasn't there yet.

On the dawn after the Battle of Bloody Ridge, more than one hundred of the soldiers of Major General Kawaguchi's crack regiment lay in front of my position, some just a few feet from my machine gun. One of them took tracer rounds that exploded in his head and I saw flames shoot from his face as it disintegrated.

It took two days to bulldoze the three thousand Japanese into mass graves. Some of them were still alive when we pushed the dirt over them.

Congress gave me their Medal of Honor for this work. Now, I was going to take it down to Fort Bragg and use it to pass through the barrier shielding a possible murderer. The more I thought about that, the more this seemed the most worthwhile thing I could do with a medal that to me felt tainted.

§

My island parasites sometimes worked a two-day cycle: the attacks, each lasting twelve hours, came at thirty-six hour intervals. A fever was coming on, and looking at my watch, I saw that it was right on schedule. I needed to find a bed.

I grabbed my duffel and walked back downtown. By the time I got there, I was doing a painful shuffle. My boots were too heavy to lift. The boardinghouse where I was expected was in a three-story brick building on a corner across the street from the auditorium. The front door was unlocked, and I went in and down a hallway running the length of the house, with a sitting room on the right and a dining room on the left, its table large enough to seat thirty and already set for the next meal.

Peg Jones, the manager, was in the kitchen at the end of the hall. As I walked in saying her name, she turned toward me.

"Welcome home, Sergeant Rollins." As she looked me over, she added, "My God, Holly! What happened to you?"

"Guadalcanal. Dropped from a hundred and sixty five to a hundred and fifteen pounds, came away with malaria and rotten lungs."

"What do you mean? What's wrong with your lungs?"

"Fungus. I cough until I spit up blood sometimes."

This conversation was starting already to make my hands shake, and I had an urge to hide them in my pockets.

Peg went on with her questions, "Were you wounded?"

"I was creased a few times."

"When are you going back?"

"Why are you asking all these questions, Peg?" I hid my hands behind my back.

"Well, Holly, there are lots of people here who want to know about you. Does Ida know you're back?"

"No. I haven't spoken to her. Have you told anybody I was coming?"

"Why should I do that?"

"Ida? Mickey?"

"Listen here, I don't mind other people's business. All right?"

"And you don't answer my questions." I raised my voice a couple of notches. "Did the Mayor or the FBI ask about me?"

"Ida came to ask if I had heard from you, a long time ago. The Mayor chases votes, and the FBI chases Nazis. They ain't gonna bother about you."

While she was talking, I was studying her face, looking for any sign she might be lying.

"If anyone at all asks about me, you never heard anything from me and don't know where I am. Okay?"

"What's wrong, Holly? Have you come back in some kind of trouble?"

She was still avoiding my questions, and she hadn't given me a key. My hands trembled and shook. My head felt like it was teetering on my neck.

"My troubles are none of your business," I said. "I want you to keep your big nose out of my affairs."

"You listen here, Cupcake! You can't come into my kitchen and speak to me like I was trash. Whatever happened to you over there, don't bring that in here. You behave or you get out."

I turned away from Peg to leave, picking up my duffel. Then she touched my arm. I dropped the duffel and jerked back. Before I could respond to this attack, I saw she was offering me a room key. I took the key, but the wariness I had about her didn't go away, and we stood there glaring at each other, Peg with her cheeks puffed out and her face red.

She raised her shoulders and lowered them again as she let a whoosh of air out through her pursed lips and said, "All right, Holly, I see what's going on here. I just have to look at you and, my God, what you must have been through. I want to help you in any way I can. God bless you, Sergeant Rollins, in these fearful times."

"Peg, I need a bed right now. All this talk can wait."

The key Peg gave me was to a room on the top floor. I had to have rest, rest, rest. As the attack came over me, the pain in my muscles shrieked their message to my brain, and I stayed in bed through the active phase of the cycle, my muscles too weak to lift me. Peg came to my room to try to bring me to the table. I yelled at her to leave me alone. She came back twice offering to bring soup. I said yes the second time and was grateful for it. Shortly afterwards I was able to fall asleep.

Later that night, I found myself on a beach where I had bulldozed a mass grave with a thousand bodies. Blood was oozing up through the sand, bubbling on the surface. I heard my own voice repeating, *Blood must be paid* over and over. I awoke from this dream with a sense of awe and dread.

The cough I had earlier returned and quickly got as bad as it had been at LaBelle's house. I went into the bathroom to take my medicine and to try soaking my head in cold water again. But this time it didn't work, and I started having convulsions and spewed blood all over the bathroom and hallway as I staggered back to my bed.

§

I awoke with a clash of images and memories flooding my brain and screams ringing in my ears. What had happened? I rushed into the hallway and saw Megan, Peg's daughter, leaning against the wall, screaming something I couldn't understand, blood spouting from her nostrils onto a floor already smeared with my own blood. Slowly, head bent forward, she lurched into the bathroom and, I assumed, to the sink to stop the bleeding. But then, a moment later she rushed out, blood still streaming, swinging a toilet plunger and began to hit me about the head and shoulders. I turned away and covered up as much as I could.

I was facing the stairway and saw Peg come running up the stairs and pass me, slipping on the blood. She still managed to grab Megan's arm and stop the pounding I was getting from the girl.

Peg kept repeating, "My God! My God!"

Megan stopped screaming long enough to say the first understandable thing I heard from her, "He smashed my nose. Son-of-a-bitch. The prom is this week."

Peg led her into the bathroom.

I was happy to get back behind my own door and to slam it shut. I sat down on the bed and tried to make sense of what was happening. I remembered running from the bathroom spewing blood all over.

Then came a vivid memory of having been asleep when a Jap sniper came and stabbed somebody. Then blood was spurting all over me, blood of a good friend of mine who died moments later. Someone grabbed my arm, and I lashed out. That must have been when I hit Megan, because the next thing I knew she was screaming and beating up on me.

This incident left me shaking and needing to go back to sleep. The door swung open and Peg came in walking stiffly, not bending her knees.

"Get your duffel packed. You're leaving. The reason I'm not calling the police is that I know this has something to do with what happened to you over there. But after this, you can't stay here. Good Lord, Holly, the girl was only trying to help you. After she saw blood all over the place."

"Tell Megan I'm sorry for what happened."

"She'll get over it. Her nose can be fixed, and there'll be other dances. But, there's something worse wrong with you, Holly, and you do need help, more than I thought."

Going downstairs a few minutes later, I was struck by the fact that I hadn't seen a single person come out into the hall to see what was going on. I knew the place was full of people. I found Peg in the kitchen on the telephone. She hung it up as I came in.

"I talked to Mickey. She and Buck will be right over. Go wait for them in front of the house."

I stood out on South Street by the curb. Buck and Mickey came in a taxi. I was happy to see them, especially since I needed their help as much as I did. They were a sister and brother who ran a boardinghouse in Asheville before the war, and I got to know them both well when I stayed there for almost a year.

Buck was about five feet six inches tall with blond hair, a sparse mustache and a hooked nose too large for his narrow face. Mickey, two inches shorter than him, had black hair with a round face and button nose. They were opposites. Where he was thin, she was stocky. Where he was nervous, she was calm. Where his hair was wavy, hers was straight, with bangs all the way around in the shape of a bowl turned upside down. Where he was like a barker in front of a sideshow, she, in her red dress, was like a fire plug in front of city hall.

The three of us took the taxi just past Five Points, not far from where they now lived, stopping at an early-morning breakfast diner. It was already five o'clock, and I was hungry. A good sign that I was mending. The railway dining car was painted brown with red trim, set back about forty feet off the street.

We had grits with thick, white gravy spread over biscuits, and served with molasses. Due to rationing, the menu didn't include the ham and eggs I wanted.

Over chicory coffee, Buck started to open up a bit. "Been a lot about you in the news. How come you're in the paper so much?"

"Buck, I can tell you one thing about the military. You know very little at any given moment, and as time goes by you know less and less. Washington gave me a medal. Maybe they're thinking to send me out on a war bond drive when I get better. Join up, Buck. You'd do okay. You always got an angle, just like they do."

Mickey said, "Pass me that molasses, Holly."

She put two spoons of it in her coffee. "I've seen people do this and wondered how it would taste."

When she tasted it, she made a face. "That's bitter," she said. "Do you remember all the trouble we had in Asheville?"

"Yes, of course I do," I replied. "How did that work out?"

Mickey gave a sideways look at Buck as she said, "It never did work out. We're still on the run from Chester's friends."

Buck cut in and said, "Chester, you mean, don't you?"

Mickey leaned toward me, away from Buck, and changed the subject. "Why did Peg throw you out in the middle of the night? Did you make a pass at her?"

With a sudden spike of anger in my chest coming into my voice, "I got fed up with her stupid questions."

Mickey looked down at her plate, and Buck sneered. I knew she was surprised by my outburst and said, "Here's the deal, Mic. Don't think of me as a nice guy. Not anymore."

"Bamboozle those clunks in Washington all you want," said Buck. "But I can see you're the same as before, except in the sugar and spice department, maybe."

"I should of known you'd be the first one to see through me, Buck."

"Smug, as always. But I like you anyways. When you used to come watch me taking suckers up in Trashville, did you ever ask why not you, when even my baby sister here could clean you out at the pool table?"

"Shut up, Buck." Mickey gave her brother a frown.

"It's okay, Mickey. Let him go on."

"Did you just get in?" Mickey asked before Buck had a chance to continue. "Have you seen any of your friends?"

"I saw LaBelle Blue."

"I know she's awful important to you."

"I'm going to try to find out about what happened to her granddaughter, Lana. Did you ever hear anything about that?"

Mickey looked down at the tabletop again while saying, "We heard about it, is all."

While Mickey and I were talking, Buck was eating his biscuit and licking molasses off his fingers. Mickey shook out her hair and used some bobby pins to fasten it.

"I got to go to work soon. Got to be in early this morning to do some cleaning before we open up. I'm working for Ida Patini now. Did you know that?"

I shook my head.

Mickey took a tiny square mirror from her purse and checked out how well she had managed her hair.

"Since she's opened her own place, half the women in town want to see her when anything special's about to happen. That place hums all day long."

Still fixing her hair, not looking at me, Mickey said, "She and Red Carter are a number. She sees him all the time now."

Without showing any response to this news, I asked Buck, "Lots of war work going on in Raleigh?"

Buck stopped sucking molasses and said, "Farms do okay. Tobacco's good. Government buys up trainloads of ciggies for the Arm' Service, so Winston-Salem and Durham done great. Training camps like Fort Bragg and Camp Lejeune. A new business took up lately is the POWs with a bunch of camps opened this year. You might even see a familiar face there, like somebody you captured, seeing you're such a hero in the funny papers."

It was time to find out what was going on with Buck.

"Okay, my friend. What's your gripe?" I said.

"You're now the great Shurluck Home. Z'at right?"

If I had been the great Sherlock, I maybe would have known what he was talking about. "What do you mean?" I asked.

"Ain't you out to knobble the man who murdered that jig you was talking about?"

"It's bad enough for you to talk about Lana like that. Don't ever talk about Labelle that way, not if you want to stay healthy. I've always got a weapon at hand that I can use in a fight."

I noticed this outburst brought an opposite reaction to the first one. This time Buck was studying his plate, and Mickey was smiling. I think she liked to see Buck get his comeuppance now and then.

Buck had his head down, now staring at the water stains on the tabletop. He looked up at me, saying, "You know, I ain't gonna fight with you, Holly. Mickey and me's come to get you cause we both always had a soft spot for you, ever since you come to live with us in Asheville when you was still just a tyke. And now here you are tough as can be, come home a hero from the roughest place on earth. I say, Thank God! Amen to that, right Mickey?"

"You said it. Amen to that," answered Mickey.

We soon finished and walked to their rented house out on Whitaker Mill Road where the houses were starting to thin out. There was a filling station and country store across the street. This was the main route to Wake Forest and beyond, and I had stopped at these places many times before the war.

Standing in front of their house I asked them, "If I get hold of a car that needs work, do you have some place to put it?"

23

Buck said, "Sure, just put it in the side yard. Where you gonna get it, the car?"

"Is there any way to rent one?"

Buck asked Mickey, "You ever heard any place like that?"

Mickey shook her head. Buck said, "I think John Deere rents trucks as well as tractors. They might rent you a pickup."

"Maybe I can find somebody who wants to sell an old heap, given the gas ration."

We went up the walk to their front door.

Mickey stopped me there, "You can't come in until I introduce you to my cat."

She opened the door and we were confronted by one of those huge tabbies with the color and almost the size of a bobcat. It coughed and growled when I came through the doorway.

Then, I swear, she said, "Joe, I want you to meet Holly. He's okay." The cat turned and wandered off the moment Mickey finished introducing me.

"How did you come to call it Joe?"

"I heard a singer on Major Bowe's Radio Amateur Hour do a song called *Don't mess with Joe* just before we adopted this feral cat. That song was a perfect fit. We live together on the understanding that he will guard the house as a favor to us, but the backyard is his alone."

Mickey showed me a bed, and I went to sleep the moment I stretched out on it.

When I woke up, they had both left the house.

§

That afternoon, I walked into Bad Dad's Hall of Pool for the first time in more than a year. The room was different from when I last saw it. There was a new chest-high counter to the right as you come in, with a cash register. Bad Dad used to give you change from a big roll he carried in his pants pockets. Behind the counter were shelves holding trays of balls. That was different, too. The balls used to just stay at home on the tables.

The place was long and narrow with just room enough for a row of crosswise tables with aisles along both walls. There were only a couple of tables working, no one hanging around looking for competition.

Bad Dad was racking balls at one of the tables. When he was done, he came towards me and said, "I read how you was the ugliest hero since Dan'l Boone. I didn't remember you that way, but now I see you look even worse'n me, just like a rack for somebody to hang a hat on."

"Well, I do remember you being big and ugly like that Chicago football player with a name like a sneeze, Bronko Nagurski."

"Gesundheit," said Bad Dad.

"Danke schoen," I replied, enjoying this familiar exchange, our private, recognition code. "You seen Buck today?"

"Buck scored a while ago and left."

"I was hoping to find him here."

While I was deciding what to do without Buck to give me a game, I began to hear an argument rising at a nearby table. One of the men had the weather-beaten but relaxed face of a tobacco farmer who hadn't started spring planting yet, still dragging out his lazy winter. He was both large and strong.

The other man's profession was just as obvious. He was an ex-pug. Probably a club fighter the way his face and head showed the results of rough fights, with a flat nose that had a left twist, cauliflower ears and eyebrows covered with scar tissue. His face was thick-skinned and his cheeks scarred by gloves doctored to rip the skin.

He looked familiar to me somehow. Then I realized it was Red Carter, a Winston-Salem high-school football and baseball player of my time.

Meanwhile, the farmer was saying to him, "If I was to hit you, I'd lay you out cold."

"Put up your money," said Red, fumbling in his pockets. He pulled out some bills and began to count them out on the pool table. "You don't get it, my sharecrop buddy. You ain't gonna hit me. Maybe if you had a ball bat."

Bad Dad, now seated behind the counter, spoke up, "Hey, Stacey! I seen him do this before. Take a cue chalk and mark two sets of footprints on the floor about three feet apart. You stand on one side, and he'll stand on the other with his hands below the waist. You try to hit him in the face."

"So, that's the bet?" asked the farmer.

"Five bucks you can't hit him in the face," said Bad Dad.

The farmer took a piece of chalk, drew the foot marks on the floor and took his position with his feet placed in two of the marks. Red looked down to place his feet in his marks. Stacey threw a left-hook at Red, trying to catch him before he looked up. Some sixth sense must have warned Red because he threw up his right arm to block the punch while still looking at the floor.

"If you're gonna be frisky, I might have to punch back," said Red.

Stacey stood glaring at Red with his arms at his side.

Red said, "Go ahead. Now you can start, unless you want to just hand over the five bucks."

Stacey looked to his left in the direction of the owner and threw a right hand at Red's face the moment he turned his head back towards Red, trying again to catch Red off-guard. I could see how useless this strategy was. He caught Red off-guard the first time, and it didn't do him any good.

It was amazing to watch Red move his upper body backwards at the pace of each punch, ending in a position looking at the fist stopped at the end of its range or swinging by an inch from his chin. And so it continued for several minutes until finally Stacey was winded and frustrated. During all this time, Red had kept his feet on his marks while his upper body seemed to move all over.

Stacey sat down on a stool, red-faced and coughing. I went over to where Red was still standing on his marks.

"Red Carter, known to the press as *Flash Gordon*."

"You know, you got that right, just like in the comic books."

"Well, let's go someplace where we can lie about the old days, when we thought we were good."

We went to a cafe next door and took a table. I ordered coffee with biscuits and gravy again.

"I can't understand why you're so beat up when you can move like you do," I told him.

26

Red looked down for a few moments before answering, "Maybe, that's how I learned those moves, Holly."

After my junior year, I left school and hadn't kept track of Red, except for the sport's page now and then.

"What happened after high school, Red?"

"I played semi-pro and pro baseball for a few years," he said, "and one summer with the Raleigh Caps. Then a friend introduced me to club boxing, where I could get fights based on my football and baseball rep. What you see is the price of on-the-job education."

"How did you know Stacey was throwing a punch at you when you were looking at the floor?"

Red cracked a smile. "You just said it, if you'll think about it." He waited a few moments for me to say something. When I didn't, he said: "I saw his feet move, shifting his weight to throw the punch."

While I was thinking over this answer, Red asked me one, "What was it like on Guadalcanal?"

"Like any tropical island but noisier."

"How do you mean?"

"Did you ever hear of the Betty?"

"Medium-range bomber?"

"Yeah. We had Bettys coming over every afternoon to bomb Henderson Field, putting craters in the runways."

Red had an eager expression on his face, involved and interested. So, I thought, what the hell, why not tell him what I can and leave out the rest.

Red said, "Where did you take your training?"

"I was trained with the Combat Engineers, and we sailed from San Francisco bay to New Zealand to do jungle training. We landed on Guadalcanal on August 7th. Australians like to say we're not jungle fighters because we start by blowing up the jungle. We don't like those Jap snipers, you see, who can be right beside you, camouflaged, without you knowing it. If you can't inhale your cigarette, maybe you've had your throat cut."

I was laying it on a bit heavy and watching the expressions on Red's face that encouraged me to go on.

"The Japs like to use noise, firecrackers in the middle of the night to keep you awake and jumpy. They use camouflage to get close and sniper fire to disrupt what you're doing. They listen in on our walkie-talkies, learn the names of our officers and give orders in perfect English. They're morale busters.

"Tents were worthless because they got beaten down by the heavy rains. We bulldozed shallow depressions in the ground to make sleeping quarters, covered with tarps that were propped up with stakes in the front, laid out flat in the back, and spread over with palm fronds on top. Thirty or forty men could sleep side by side in each one of these.

"Sometimes when the men were asleep, a sniper would infiltrate these quarters, stab two or three men, roll out and get away. Now, all of us had knives or bayonets. When we heard the wounded screaming, each man would huddle up as tight as he could in the dark, and when somebody touched him, he'd lunge back at 'em with his knife."

"That's hard to imagine," said Red.

I felt like I maybe could get the hang of this story-telling, but that was enough for one day.

After that, the rest of the afternoon did me good, hearing Red going on about things I could play back in my memory. As I listened to him talk about games we had both been in before all the craziness of the past year, I felt like I wanted to go over every game and argue about every big play. But eventually, Red had to leave, and I walked back across town to Buck and Mickey's. Thoughts of Ida came into my mind during this walk, but each time they jumped right out again as though they had landed on a hot stove.

§

I got off the bus at the Fort Bragg gate to do the one thing for LaBelle no one else could do. I was in uniform and wearing a blue ribbon around my neck supporting the Medal of Honor that I hoped would get me in to see the General commanding the Fort.

I offered my papers to an MP Corporal.

Without looking at my papers he said, "Good morning, Sergeant Rollins, welcome to Fort Bragg."

No, I wasn't wearing a name tag. He knew me because I was wearing the medal. I asked the Corporal to direct me to base headquarters. He turned, leaned to put his head through the window of the guard shack, and yelled, "Private, come out here double-quick to take Sergeant Rollins to Base HQ."

The medal had more pull than I thought. In no time at all, I was admitted to the office of Brigadier General Lawrence Fishbinder. As I approached his desk, the General leaped to his feet and threw me a salute. I wasn't surprised because this same thing had happened in Washington. I returned the salute.

"This is the first time in my career I've saluted a Medal of Honor man," gruffed the General. "Good work, Sergeant." General Fishbinder sat down and waved me to take a seat directly in front of his desk. "What can I do for you, Sergeant?"

"Sir, I am here on an unusual and personal mission. A young woman was murdered in Raleigh, a woman related to someone very dear to me. I came here to use my Medal of Honor to help her, to gain access to you and to ask your permission to speak with Sergeant Boyd, who may have some knowledge of this murder, Sir."

"Sergeant, I appreciate your honesty," the General paused and then said, "Since you have been direct and honest with me, I will be equally honest with you. I cannot let you speak with Sergeant Boyd, but I will have a stenographer copy the transcript of Boyd's interview by the Post JAG Officer. I hope that will do because it is all I can offer."

"General, Sir, I will be very pleased to have a copy of that transcript."

"In that case, Sergeant, return to my office this afternoon, and my secretary will give it to you." Before he had a chance to move I was on my feet, whipped him off a snappy salute, and left his office.

At dinner that evening at the NCO Club, I took the transcript from the yellow manila folder the secretary had given me and read it. In summary, the Sergeant told the interviewer that he had known Lana as the best friend of Marla Brown. It was Marla he went to see, frequently at Lana's cabin, one of the few places they could meet, given segregation in North Carolina. The last time he saw either of the two girls was the week before Lana was killed. He spent Saturday with the two of them and dropped them off at a place on South Street, a grocery store that turned into a local bar as soon as it got dark. He remembered speaking with the bartender, a man named Leroy Struthers.

There was an affidavit from a Captain Braddock, an enlistment officer in Raleigh. Per instructions received from the JAG office, he had interviewed Leroy Struthers at the store on South Street. Struthers remembered the girls because of the color combination of Lana Blue and Marla Brown. He also spoke with Sergeant Boyd who had been there several times before that evening. Captain Braddock interviewed Lana's father Mose Blue as well, who confirmed Boyd's story in every detail.

JAG was of the opinion that Boyd's story was correct. They recommended that no further action be taken and that he not be turned over to civilian authorities for questioning, since they might hold him in jail, interfering with his training.

Even an amateur like me could see a big open question after reading the JAG report. Where was he at the time Lana was murdered? And, did he go to Raleigh the weekend of the murder?

Also, LaBelle wanted me to find out if Boyd knew of anybody involved with Lana. Why not be guided by the experts? The JAG had sent a local person in Raleigh to do some snooping for them. I could do the same. I was going to hire an agency to find out when Sergeant Boyd was in Fayetteville. Since I couldn't see him on base, I'd see him when he was on a pass off-base.

The following morning, I went to the front desk of the NCO's club to get a Fayetteville telephone directory. The idea of using a local detective appealed to me.

Along with the directory, I was handed a note from Sergeant Boyd telling me that he wanted to meet at noon in town at a private, Airborne-only, topless club called the *Tat-for-Tit*. Damn, that was easy. Maybe this wasn't going to be a tough as I thought.

§

Fayetteville was new to me and, maybe, new to everybody. The tens of thousands of young men in training at Fort Bragg had attracted a carnival atmosphere to the town. There were shooting galleries and peep shows all along Main Street. There were games offering kewpie doll prizes and grifters on street corners running three-card monte scams. If you can't find the queen, try looking at the guy's palm and don't pay any attention to the other man who just won big. He's the shill bringing in suckers like you.

Even though it was Thursday morning and not a weekend, there were thousands of soldiers on the sidewalks. Almost all of them had very short hair, darkly tanned faces and new uniforms. All shoulders, chests and sleeves were bare, except for a few sharpshooter badges, since none of them had any marks of rank or service.

At the door of the club, I explained that I was meeting Sergeant Boyd and was shown to his table.

He greeted me with, "I heard you read the JAG records and thought it might be a good idea for us to talk. Have a seat. Tell me what it is you want to know."

"Tell me about Lana Blue, what you knew about her," I said, taking a chair across from him.

"It's funny you ask me about Lana. I barely knew her. She was Marla's friend, and we used to meet sometimes at her place out by the creek, but that's all."

"How did you meet Marla?"

Before he had a chance to answer, a waitress leaned over to ask if I wanted a drink. She had all the equipment you would expect with nothing left to the imagination. This was a new experience for me and I wasn't sure where to look. But the more I tried not to look at her chest, the more my eyes were drawn there. Then, I woke up to the understanding that I was in a topless bar. You're supposed to look. With that, I gave her equipment a motor-pool inspection and confirmed that everything looked to be in good shape and in the right places.

I mumbled an order and she relieved my stress by going off to fill it.

"Tell me, Sergeant," Boyd said, "what do you want? I don't think it's a play-by-play story. You want to know if I did it. Isn't that right?"

"I don't care about the details, unless you tell me something I find hard to believe."

"Wait here, Sergeant, I'll be right back. There's someone I want you to meet." With that, he left the table, going toward the back of the large room.

While waiting for him to come back, I looked around for the first time. It was afternoon and the natural light gave the place a tired and worn-out appearance, like an old carnie stripper when you see her on the boardwalk without her make-up. There were maybe a dozen soldiers dancing with young women and maybe another dozen young women dancing with each other.

Speaking of strippers, when the half-naked waitress came with my drink, I found I wasn't yet a seasoned *Tat-for-Tit* man. I paid for my drink with her again just a few inches away. I decided that the secret was just to accept her equipment as a natural part of the scenery. I felt better having at last worked this out.

Boyd came back to the table with a young woman. "Sergeant, this is Doris." Turning to Doris, he said, "Tell him what you know about Marla Brown."

Doris told me what she knew, and it wasn't that much. But it was enough. Boyd started seeing Doris two weeks before Lana was murdered. He told her about Marla and that he had stopped seeing Marla because she was just a flirt and gold digger.

But the main thing Doris had to say was that the weekend that ended with Lana being murdered was their first weekend together. Doris said she wasn't going to forget that, especially now that they were engaged.

I thought over Doris' story and had nothing to ask her. Turning to Boyd I asked, "Did you ever meet any of Lana's friends? I mean any men she was seeing."

"No," he said, "she seemed to be going through a bad time. I couldn't figure it out. Too much booze, maybe."

I thanked both of them for their time and cooperation.

Boyd came back with a question of his own, "Marla didn't point a finger at me, did she?"

"Not as far as I know. Why?"

"I don't think I meant much to her. She was serious about somebody else."

"Thanks, I'll look into that. Now, I want to finish up here, and I've thought of another question for you. Why didn't you talk to the police? You didn't have anything to worry about."

"The police never tried to talk to me, that I know of."

"I heard the 82nd wouldn't let the police talk to you."

"Sergeant Rollins, you know better than me that the army's gonna do what they're gonna do. They're not gonna ask my opinion about it. Maybe they didn't care one way or another."

"Care about what?"

"The army isn't a party, not even a Boston Tea Party. Heartless killers are welcome here."

Feeling I now knew everything I needed to know about Sergeant Hoppy Boyd, I caught an afternoon bus back to Raleigh.

§

There was a wind blowing when I arrived on Fontaine Street. Price's truck wasn't there again today. I walked through flapping, wet sheets to LaBelle's front door. It was already a warm day before noon, and her front door was open. As I came into the house, I could see her bending over a wash tub on her back porch. It was hot and humid inside and, as I passed the stove I could see why. There were three large pots of water releasing steam into the air. As I came out onto the porch I could see the hot water barrel was already half full.

Passing around the barrel, I stepped down a few of the back stairs and turned around to face LaBelle. As she looked up at me, I said, "I have news about Sergeant Boyd."

Without speaking, she gestured to me to follow her, turned and walked into the kitchen.

I followed her and, for the second time in my life, I saw LaBelle take a seat at her kitchen table and motion me to sit opposite her. I couldn't help but think I was being given a treat, even in all this heat and humidity that felt like I was back on Guadalcanal and made me wonder if my germs would wake up again.

"I went to Fort Bragg and, like you suggested, used my medal to get to see the commanding officer. It kind of worked and kind of didn't work."

"How do you mean?" she had her usual patient and attentive expression.

The sweat was starting to tickle as it rolled down my chest and burning where it was seeping into the corners of my eyes. I had seen animated newsreels of gremlins attacking airplanes and tanks in the factories. I was beginning to picture germs working on my innards

33

in that way. I looked over at LaBelle who still seemed to be coolly waiting for me to get to the point.

"The general refused my request to speak with Boyd. But he did offer me a copy of the entire file of their investigation. I accepted his offer, given that it was all I was going to get anyway. Here is the file his secretary gave me."

I handed the file I had brought back from Fort Bragg to LaBelle.

"I'm sure you've read it. Tell me what it says."

"I think their investigation was good, but I also saw the man himself off-base and learned some things from him.

"First, he wasn't interested in Lana but in her friend Marla.

"Second, the last time he saw the girls was a few weeks before what happened to Lana.

"Third, and this is the clincher. He didn't come to Raleigh during that weekend. He was with a new woman who confirms that story."

LaBelle didn't seem disappointed. "So, Boyd didn't kill Lana." she said. Her reaction made me think she wasn't really convinced it was him in the first place.

"Did you think it was him, or did you suspect someone else all along?"

"I think Lana was murdered. After that, I don't think because I don't know anything. That's why I wanted you to find out. If it wasn't him, who was it?"

"Tatie, I have no idea. And clearly I'm not the one to find out who did it. I don't know how to do that. I'll tell the police what I learned about this Boyd character, and then we need to leave it to them."

"Moon, the police aren't going to find anything. Even a beautiful girl like Lana is just a waste of time to them when she's colored."

"You can't expect me to do anything more, Tatie."

"Listen to me, Moon. I know you will find the man."

"If you know that, why not tell me who it was and be done with it?"

"Don't be sassy. I've told you how I feel about this. Now, you need to do the rest."

"I have no idea where to start."

"Okay. I can see that. Before, we had a name and someplace to go. Now, we don't know anything about who the man is or where to look for him. You got one choice left, Moon. Go find out about Lana. What was she doing and who with?"

I began to squirm. What with the heat and my malaria and the fungus in my lungs getting happy as I expected and the pressure to find out what I had no means to find out, I was getting worse than sassy. There was a wall rising that separated me from LaBelle.

"Tatie, I can't do all that."

"Okay, I understand. I'll just ask you to do only one thing. Talk to the police. If there's time later on, you might go talk to Mose. Maybe he knows something without knowing what it means. He might even know where Jerome is at. I don't expect he'd tell me."

"All right, Tatie. I don't want to let you down if I can do something. I'll go talk to them soon."

The one thought that was clear to me as I was getting ready to leave was that I needed help. LaBelle wasn't going to give up.

My back was turned to the open door. I heard a laugh and then a high-pitched voice coming from the porch behind me, "How d'ja like t'be a waugh HEEro?"

I turned to see LaBelle's son, Mose Blue, a large man of about sixty with short white hair. He pushed through the doorway as though he had to force his way into the house. He had that intent, very serious but unfocused expression on his face of someone who is well and truly drunk. He brushed me aside to continue into the house.

LaBelle blocked his path and said, "Mose, I told you not to come here acting up like this."

Mose almost walked into her but stopped just in time and stood before her, head tilted back as though he was talking directly to God himself.

"You mind me now, Ol' Mammy. Bedda be nice."

LaBelle grabbed his arm, "Mose, you're too big to come here talking ugly like this. I'm sure you think it's funny, but that's because you're drunk."

Mose pulled his arm away, straightened his shoulders, rising to his full height and glory. He was a big man, six foot four or more.

35

Speaking in his normal, deep voice, he said, "I am big and I think big." Mose raised his right arm and flexed a huge muscle. "All night poker game at my place and people drunk. But not me. I own the place, see." Mose lowered his arm. "Don't matter what you think, I ain't drunk. I'm the boss."

LaBelle stared at him for several seconds, then stepped aside to let him enter as she said, "Yeah, come in, Boss, I don't want you wandering around on my street like a drunk, crazy man. But don't pass out until you say where Jerome is at."

He sat down by the table, put his head down and said in a muffled voice, "Jerome is as was, and ever will be. Amen! In his Godly Place, unto himself."

"Listen, you need to stay awake a little bit more. Did he come get Lana's body and see to her being buried?"

Mose raised his head to look at LaBelle.

"Why'r'ya askin' me?" he said. "I didn't have nothing to do with it, and I don't know where Jerome is at."

"And I don't know where Lana's body is now. You had everything to do with that, since you were the one who identified her at the morgue."

Mose said, "That's true. But, why talk about Jerome? The Mighty Holiness is too busy makin' money for The Lord to worry about Lana."

"You tell me what happened, then. Do the police still have her body?"

"Don't know."

For the first time as long as I had known her, she let her face slip for a moment and suddenly looked old and tired. Without tears, but with eyes that glistened and were fixed in a stare, she said, "Mose, where is she? Why didn't you do nothing? Why didn't Jerome come and help?"

Mose responded without looking up, "He's your grandson. Why don't you ask him?"

"I told you, I don't know where he's at. Dammit, Mose, why didn't you take care of all this?"

Mose left his chair and went into the bedroom.

"You're not getting off that easy." The commanding tone in her voice mounted even higher as she continued, "Get Lana's body and arrange a funeral."

The moment had passed. LaBelle's face regained the serenity I was used to seeing there.

She said, "Mose talks about truth, but when everything floats in liquor, truth is that truth don't mean nothing. We need to see poor Lana buried. Somebody's got to go back to that place where he saw Lana's body to see if she's still there, or can we find where she's at now."

Without a doubt, this whole thing was now mine alone. I needed to get help, somebody healthy and reliable.

Chapter Two

*Military leadership is a process by which a soldier
influences others to accomplish the mission.*

----Combat Leader's Field Guide

Friday March 5, 1943

On a hunch that this was one of Red's regular days to practice
his hit-me grift, I sat for several hours in front of the Hall of Pool
waiting for him to show up, enjoying the warmth of the day and
watching the comings and goings across the street. A boy in his late
teens crossed over from that side and walked past me, then came
back and stopped where he blocked my view.

"Aren't you from Guadalcanal? With the Medal?" Next, he
asked for my autograph.

Since he was too young to be weaned but old enough to be
drafted, I wrote in the margin of his newspaper, on the sports page,
'When your draft number comes up, good luck and I hope you get
a good view of the war. Holly Rollins, Platoon Sergeant, First
Battalion, Combat Engineers.'

I went back to my quiet study of the doings across the street,
this time watching a horse-drawn milk-delivery wagon. I watched
the man as he took milk and butter from the wagon and put them
on a front porch while the horse lowered his head and dragged the
wagon to the next house, stopped, and waited. The horse did the
same when the man went off again, except he passed three houses
before stopping. I watched the man make deliveries to two of these
and skip the last one as he came back to the wagon to pick up more
milk and butter. Along the next block as far as I was able to see
them, they sometimes passed over one or more houses, and they
sometimes did one or more deliveries in a single loop. It seemed
they each knew the route and did their part independently, but it was
the horse who continued to lead the way by being the first at each
of these stops. It all made me wonder what would happen if the dairy
ever decided to switch to a van.

This was my day to enjoy animals. A sharecropper's wagon rolled by piled with sacks bearing the name of a local feed and seed emporium, pulled by a grunting, farting mule worn down by plowing and the effort to pull home these heavy seed bags.

I was still exercising my noodle over the big question of milk-deliveries when the wagon passed again, going in the other direction, now emptied of its milk and butter. This time, the horse showed how much he wanted to get to the barn, high-stepping the wagon along with his head up, making his hooves clop and clop on the soft, warm tar. From his point of view, I guess, there's nothing to compare with the attraction of stall and feedbag.

Just when I was about to leave, up came Red and silently dropped down into the wicker chair next to mine. I decided to prolong my peaceful moment.

Red lit up a corncob with a blackened bowl that was burnt through in places, not unusual in a pipe with a soft bowl.

I asked him, "Do you think smoking's bad for you?"

"No sir, I don't care to."

"Nor me, neither. I worked two tobacco harvests when I was a boy. When you see and smell it curing in the barn, it's hard to believe. It comes out soft like buckskin, smelling sweet and smoky at the same time. Hard to believe anything this good could hurt you."

"Not a pipe, anyway. Some smokes, like cigarettes, I'm not sure about. Did you ever hear how they hack, the people who smoke them things?"

"I saw a Model-T pass a minute ago," I said, changing the subject. "Back one time my father owned a Model-T truck and claimed that small engine was easy on fuel. You think the gas ration brought 'em back?"

"Don't know. When I was a boy, everybody who had one said the same as your father."

It was time to get on with what I came for.

"Red, I need some help, and I'd be happy if you'd be able to give me a hand."

"What doing?"

"Helping out on my chores."

"Billy Sunday put up a tent since the last time you had chores to do."

I raised my voice sharply, "How come nobody knows anymore how to answer a simple, damn question?"

"Okay, calm down and I'll answer when I understand the question. As far as my time is concerned, my fight money's out there doing its job, so you could call me semi-retired and available."

"Okay, Red, but I guess I don't understand. If you got money, why do you do that dumb hustle of yours?"

"I don't like chumps, and I don't mind telling you my grub tastes better when I buy it with chump money."

We sat in silence again, and it boiled down to three things. First, on the field he was the most capable person I ever saw and a good man to have on your side. Second, I didn't like that he was a hustler and wondered if he could be trusted, but I could certainly watch him. Third, LaBelle's need was greater than my doubt. I decided to go ahead and pitch it to him.

"LaBelle Blue needs to find out about Lana, but I'm not physically up to it. I need help to get it done, and it's something worth doing."

"Find out what about Lana?"

"What happened? How come she was murdered? Who did it? Maybe, most important, where's her body? Seems like that got lost."

"Okay, that's worth doing. LaBelle can count on me to help out."

"By the way, I don't believe I asked if you know anything about this murder yourself."

"Do you have a plan, Holly?"

"My idea's to talk to the police and follow up on what they know. LaBelle thinks we should track Lana's backtrail, who she did what with. We need to do both. How does that sound?"

"Okay. Before we go ahead with this, I've got a question for you."

"Fire away."

"Well, you and Ida were an item before the war. I don't know what happened, and I'm not asking. But I want to know how you feel about me being with Ida now."

The question annoyed me, yet it was a fair request.

"I wouldn't call that a correct history, Red. We were not an item. Could be, we were about to be before the war and while I was in boot camp. After I went overseas, we stopped writing and that was all there was to it."

"Holly, I don't want to push you. But, if we're going to work together, you need to answer my question directly. How do you feel about me and Ida being together?"

"I feel okay about it. If ever I change my mind, you'll be the first to hear."

"Fair enough. You asked awhile back what I know about Lana. I used to see her at that store on South Street where she hung out with a friend of hers, named Marla."

"You went down there? Were you welcome?"

"One Saturday night I was out escorting a bottle around town and ended up resting, as you might say, on the grass in front of the auditorium. A soldier woke me up and offered to take me to a place downtown where you could get a drink late at night. Off we went, and after that I went there often. The people there seemed to get used to me hanging around.

"Lana worked in that store when she was a kid. Not in the bar, of course. She stopped when she went to live with LaBelle. Not long ago, I did see her there a few times with Marla."

As I listened to Red, I was surprised that LaBelle hadn't mentioned anything about Lana's history over there. She probably didn't realize the connection.

"I need to go get some rest now, but I'd like to hear all you know about this, Red. Everything you're saying is new to me."

Red looked at me with a grin, like he was a buzzard, and I was road kill, "For an investigator, you don't know much. I see why you need help."

"Red, one thing I do know is that we need to make a visit to that store. I already had an idea to talk with the bartender, Leroy Struthers, after hearing about him at Fort Bragg."

"Good plan, Holly. When we go down there, I'd like to bring Ida along. I've told her about that place before, and she's always wanted to give it a look-see. She thinks it would be dangerous and exciting to go to an all-night, all-black bar."

"Okay. How about tomorrow, Saturday? Does that work?" I said as I stood up, ready to go get some sleep.

Red said he'd let Ida know, and we agreed on eleven as a time to pick her up.

"By the way, before you go, I've been meaning to ask you. How is Powell Reddy? I know you guys were great pals, and I heard you were together overseas."

I sat down at a table across from Red, taking a moment to get my thoughts together, to deal with a big subject.

"Powell was killed during the Bloody Ridge battle, I'm sorry to say."

"Damn, me too. I'm surprised you didn't mention that when you were telling me the stuff that happened over there."

It is strange his name hadn't come up then, or earlier when we were talking sports. Powell had been there when we played those games. "What do you want to know, Red? I know you liked Powell."

"Just what happened to him, Holly?"

"Powell and I were together on a machine gun during that battle. He was killed when a grenade landed just behind us and went off when he picked it up."

"So he was killed instantly. Is that right?"

Suddenly, I heard a loud ringing inside my head. It was like being inside a bass drum pounded on with a heavy mallet. Sometimes my malaria attacks started out like this. I put my hand over my ears and noticed the alarm beginning to appear on Red's face. Then, I was flung backwards in my chair as though the back of the chair had been yanked by a Hercules. The chair went over and my shins smacked the bottom of the table hard enough to spill everything onto Red. I went down hard with the noise still pounding in my head and passed out as I hit the floor.

§

A crack of white light came in from the edges of my field of vision. That light slowly opened toward the center until my entire visual field was full of light, and I became aware that I could see.

Red was sitting beside me, and we were in a hospital emergency room with an open curtain and nurses and doctors passing by. "Are you all right?"

43

"No," was all I could manage, and I was proud to be able to say that.

"Did you have an epileptic fit? Is that what happened?"

"Doannoh, Red," I said softly.

My shins were aching where I banged them into the table.

I said, "Nee rest," a little clearer this time.

A nurse came along, saw I was awake, and made Red go out to the waiting room. She told me they were going to keep me under observation for a few hours, and I should sleep if I could.

As I lay there waiting to fall asleep, I couldn't help but wonder. Nothing like this had ever happened to me before. As I mulled it over, I watched two motorcycle policemen come in and speak to the nurse at the desk in the center of the large room. She pointed at me and one of them came over and took up a position at the foot of my bed. The other one left the room.

The second policemen soon returned. He was followed by a small man wearing a seersucker suit with rolled-up trousers over canary-yellow cowboy boots, a bowler hat and a bowtie matching his boots. He hustled along with bounding, quick steps and crossed the emergency room in two seconds flat.

"Sergeant Holly Rollins, hero on the run, happy to greet you at last. My name is Battle Washburn, Mayor of the City of Raleigh. Call me 'Mayor Bats'. My friends call me that, even the ones who don't think I'm crazy. Did you get any of the messages I left for you in Washington?"

"Not run'n," I mumbled. "On a mission."

"Well, my boy, I'm a man who believes in scratching what itches. When quid pro quos are in order, your mission shall be my mission."

"Lana Blue, black woman, murdered. Want information."

With no hesitation, the Mayor said, "You shall be informed." He whipped out a business card and put it down on a table by the bed. "Call this number and talk with my secretary. She'll give you a letter to take to the Chief of Police. Is that everything?"

"No, need car, gas to see people."

"Not a deal-breaker, but it may have to be an old car, even an old truck. Given the car shortage, you'll have to take what nobody else wants."

"How do I get it?"

"Go to the City Garage to pick it up, and when you see my secretary, she'll make sure you get a city ration card along with the letter to the Chief. Does this cover it?"

"Believe it does, Mayor. Grateful for your help."

"There is a price," said the Mayor. "I want to ride with you in a parade down Fayetteville Street Saturday week, at two o'clock in the afternoon. We haven't had one damn thing to celebrate in this war and one helluva lotta things to mourn. Now, we are going to celebrate the first Medal of Honor awarded to someone from Raleigh."

"Parade, sure, you got it."

The Mayor shook my hand to seal the bargain. Then he said, "You can have one or two members of your family come with us, if you'd like. I mean one or two in our limo. There could be others in other cars."

"Yes, I have a friend I want to ride in the limousine with me."

"No problem, who is that?"

"Her name is LaBelle Blue."

"Is she related to Lana Blue, the murdered woman you just asked me about?"

"Grandmother."

"So, she's a Negro woman?"

"Correct."

"Well, Sergeant. That's no problem. I'll have a car following ours with some State and City people, including some Negro employees. She can ride with them."

"In the limo with me."

"The art of the possible is the name of the game. I'll use one of our Negro chauffeurs and she can ride up front sitting next to him."

"As you say, Mayor Bats, the art of the possible."

"We have a deal," replied the Mayor.

Having gotten what he came for, Mayor Bats went over to the nurse's station and had a happy time chatting up doctors and nurses for a few minutes. Then he was gone in a sudden burst of energy.

§

In the morning, a nurse's aide woke me with a breakfast tray of powered eggs, spam, and grits. I took one look and said, "I hate to be childish, but I don't want spam. Take that tray away and just bring me some cereal."

"This is all there is. But you don't have to eat it." With that she whipped the tray away and left me hungry. As she left she said over her shoulder, "You have visitors."

A minute later, Red came in and sat down on the edge of my bed. "Ida Patini insisted on coming along. I'm not sure how you feel about that. Is it all right if she comes in?"

I didn't really want to see her but here she was.

"Okay," I told Red. "That's all right."

He went out to get her and, as they came into the room, Ida said in a bright voice, "I've heard you look like a case of Yellow River famine."

She stopped at the door, and Red stopped behind her. She stood there quietly for a long moment. In a soft, lower tone, "Sorry, I didn't imagine you would be so……destroyed."

"Hey," I said. "The winner is the one still standing at the bell."

A physician walked past them and came over to me. With his best bedside mumble, he shared the knowledge that, though he had no idea what was wrong with me, something surely was. He suggested I stay for tests, such as a detailed, blood work-up. I gave him my best GI answer. "I'll go on sick call when I get back to the base."

He left and Red and Ida approached.

They were just out of earshot during the conversation with the physician. Red asked, "Nothing too terminal, I hope. You got enough on your plate just being Holly."

"What did he tell you?" Ida asked in a calm and even tone, standing hip-to-hip with Red at the foot of the bed.

"Take two aspirin and call in the morning."

Since the hospital couldn't figure out what was wrong with me, I decided to leave. Red agreed to waste some gas on me and dropped me off at a city garage downtown. The car the Mayor promised was a battered, Model-A Ford in need of serious attention. I managed to coax it along as far as Buck and Mickey's and to put it out of the way in their side yard.

I worked on the car that afternoon. It had been up on blocks with its tires wrapped in tar paper. I pumped them up at a filling station and used a ration card I found in the glove box to get three gallons of gas. The A didn't start right away, but there was a slight grade to the drive of the filling station. I gave it a shove and jumped in. It started after rolling after about two feet. You can't keep a Model-A down.

I decided to take a run over to LaBelle's to let her know we were going to the store to talk to Leroy.

After we had covered that, I said, "Now, I need to ask you for a favor. The Mayor is giving a parade in my honor next week. I want you to be there with me."

"I'll come watch the parade, of course."

"No, Tatie, I want you to be in the parade with me."

LaBelle nodded her head. "All right," she said.

"Great, I'll let you know the details as soon as I can."

With that I left to go rest until it was time for our night patrol to visit the store.

§

Another nightmare, this time one I couldn't remember, woke me from my nap. As I lay there in the darkness I heard the slight scrape of a Jap sniper's boot. He was crawling up to me as I lay motionless, hardly breathing through my wide-open mouth, waiting for him to make another mistake. I needed dirt or something to stuff into my mouth so he wouldn't hear me breathing.

The soft light of a full moon was coming through the window. As I studied a shadow, it changed from jungle foliage to a dresser and back to jungle foliage again.

I waited for the Jap to make his move and fell asleep still waiting.

It seemed only a moment later when my alarm clock went off, and it was time to get back to being Shurluck Home. I especially liked the *luck* part of the name Buck gave me.

I wiped the early dew off the Model-A and went to pick up Ida at her place on Jones Street. Just as I stopped in front of her place, she came out.

"What a junker." she commented as she got into the A.

I let that pass, as I was trying to adjust to her fashion statement as Cab Calloway's Minnie the Moocher.

She was wearing a bright yellow, polka-dot blouse with dots the size of silver dollars and a knee-length black skirt with yellow stripes. She had on black, low-heel shoes with yellow socks. To top it off, she was wearing a yellow bandana wrapped around her head similar to the Sheik of Araby but for the two ends sticking out like goat horns.

"What is this outfit you're wearing?" I managed to gasp.

"I'm just trying to fit in, wear something appropriate. This would be terrific in Yonkers."

"This ain't Yonkers and you ain't Satin Sadie."

"I went to a lot of trouble to put this together and I'm going to wear it, if only this one night."

Ida can be firm, and she spoke now in that decided manner that leaves no room for debate.

I blurted, "Red told me you thought this might be dangerous. Now I can see why."

We hurtled off rack-clack-rack-clack at twenty-five miles an hour. We went through town center and lurched onto South Street at Shaw, the leading black University of North Carolina. First, we had to go west to pick up Red, who lived a few blocks west of the auditorium and just off South Street.

Red got into the rumble seat, saying "Nice outfit, ready for a night of jazz."

"Red, I'm wondering about this gas rationing, I mean how that works. Can you get by on your ration? I'm assuming you do use that car you had yesterday."

"No, I keep it in storage mostly. I have a motorcycle and an airplane that takes all my ration plus black market gas to get to my fights."

We went back down South Street, heading east. The tar ended two blocks past the auditorium, and we were on a dirt road. There were no streetlights in this neighborhood, though we were still downtown.

The rack-clack of the A resounded off the dwellings we were passing. In the moonlight, many of them looked like LaBelle's place, shacks of unpainted wood turned black with age. Several of these shacks had Cadillac automobiles parked on the bare earth of the front or side yard.

We arrived at the store and I shut down the A. The place was dark with no other vehicles parked nearby. We could hear music and loud voices in the quiet of the night. We walked around the store. There were no windows but there was a ribbon of light around the back door. When I opened it, we heard a terrific din coming from the thirty or more people inside. As we walked toward the bar, everyone stopped talking with all eyes on Ida's costume.

The bartender was standing inside the store while everyone else was in an addition, a twenty by twenty foot room. You could see that the bar had been added by the simple means of cutting away a section of the top half of the back wall of the store and nailing a plank to the bottom of that cut-out section.

The room was completely quiet as we ordered beers. We were given unopened bottles of Pabst by the bartender. Bottle openers were nailed to the front of the bar every foot or two, with piles of bottle caps on the dirt floor. We opened our beers, made vague toasting gestures, and took a swig. As though that had been the signal for festivities to recommence, whispered conversations started up on all sides. Only those standing near us at the bar remained silent.

"I'm looking for Leroy Struthers," I said to the bartender who was still standing across the bar from us. The moment these words were out of my mouth, I realized both that this was, in fact, Leroy, and that I knew him.

"How come you be looking for Leroy?"

"Cut it out, Leroy. I know it's you, and I know you're the only bartender who works this place."

Leroy looked blankly at me. "Do you know Leroy, Mister? Cause I think you don't know Leroy."

"How about Dad's Bowling Alley, Leroy?"

"You talkin' bout your daddy?"

"I'm talking about you being a pain-in-the-butt pin-setter at Dad's bowling alley. Ring any bells?"

"What bells?"

"How about me yelling: 'Leroy, quit playing Tonk and get out on alley 6.' You remember that?"

"No."

"You know how I remember you, Leroy? You were the one I had to come find when I wanted you to work."

"What you want now?"

"Do you know Lana Blue?" I asked Leroy.

"Why you wanna know?"

"LaBelle Blue asked me to come see you." I had hoped he might react to Lana's name, but it was the mention of LaBelle that got a reaction.

"Wha'zat?" Leroy seemed confused for just a moment and then he visibly puffed himself up. "That ain't right. Miz LaBelle wanna talk to me, the boss woulda told me."

"So, did you know Lana or not?"

"I kinda know her," Leroy admitted in a lowered voice, rubbing a rag on the bar.

"Didn't an Army officer come in here and ask you about her?"

Now it was Leroy's turn to stare back at me.

"A man come in one night asking did I see Lana with that soldier from Fort Bragg."

Now we had come to the question I had come here to ask him.

"Since that night, have you seen either of those girls, Lana or Marla?"

"They come in sometime. They ain't here tonight."

"When was the last time you saw either one of them?"

"Las' week, I think."

"And who was that you saw?"

"They both here las' week."

Leroy began to move down the bar, mopping it with his dirty rag.

I couldn't think of anything else to ask him. We left our half-empty bottles on the bar and went back out the door. As we walked around the store, the noise inside increased until, by the time we reached the Model-A, it was as loud as when we arrived.

"Why did he lie?" Red asked me as we drove off. "He said he saw Lana last week."

"That's a clue," said Ida. "He gave himself away!"

"That could be right," I said. "But it could be that he saw Marla here last week and just assumed that Lana was with her."

"What was all that stuff about Dad?" asked Ida. "I thought that's where you went to shoot pool."

"The other half of his building is a bowling alley. When I was about fifteen, he gave me a job running that place four nights a week. Leroy was one of the pin-setters. He wanted to make money on Tonk. So, when I'd call him to set pins, he wouldn't do it until, finally, I'd have to go back and all but drag him out."

"What's Tonk?" Red asked.

"It's a game between poker and gin rummy with only five cards that you draw to from the stack. You can throw down your cards any time and win the pot if you have the most points."

"How much money did Leroy make setting pins?" Red asked. "An hour."

"He made a nickel a line. A party of four, let's say, might take about an hour to bowl a game. That would be twenty cents to Leroy, paid at closing time."

"No wonder he liked Tonk," said Ida.

The car seemed twice as loud at night, waking up the neighborhood as we passed through. I turned off South Street onto Fayetteville Street, driving down Raleigh's main street for the first time since well before the war. This was not a late city, and it was locked up tight.

Assuming they were not informed, I told them, "This is the route of the parade. It's going to start behind the Capitol building and come down to the auditorium."

We drove through town and were almost all the way back at Ida's place, ready to drop her off, when she said, "Go see Marla and ask her what happened. As far as we know, she could even be a witness to the murder."

"You're right. But I'll talk to the police first. We don't know much about what happened, so we need to find out what the police know. Including what they may know about how to find Marla."

§

The Mayor told me to stop by his office to pick up the letter to the Chief of Police. I decided to drive down because I wanted to stop by and get Red on the way.

At the Mayor's office, I left Red in the car and went to see the secretary. When I walked into her office, she stood up. Placing both her hands on top of the desk and leaned forward revealing several of her charms and said, "When the Mayor told me you were coming, I broke my bra strap jumping around in my excitement."

I could see how much she needed the support.

"You know," said the young woman still giving me the full effect of her endowment and her big peepers. "With all the men overseas, a woman today can't let her chances pass her by, if you know what I mean."

I noticed the golden band on a finger of her left hand. "And your husband is......where?"

"Why, Sweetheart, he took your job over there, and I thought you might take his job over here."

"Someday, when I'm sitting in a foxhole full of misery, I'm going to replay this conversation in my mind and be filled with regret."

"Here's your letter and ration card, Hot Stuff. I've attached a card with my telephone number, in case that longing strikes before you leave town. Don't be lonely when you don't have to be."

That sounded like something Sinatra might sing. On that note, I said, "Thanks for the memories," as I walked out.

The police station was across the street, and Red and I went in together.

The Desk Sergeant took the letter in to the Chief, and soon we were ushered into his office.

The Chief was reading the letter when we came in. He asked, "What is it you're trying to find out, Sergeant?"

"Chief, LaBelle Blue is the grandmother of the Blue girl who was murdered recently. She believes the investigation got bogged down when Sergeant Boyd couldn't be questioned by the police. She just wants to get an idea of what's going on."

The Chief picked up his phone to find out who was handling the Blue investigation and arranged for me to see a Lieutenant Cabot. As we were leaving his office he shook my hand and said, "Thanks for your sacrifice, Sergeant. I'm honored to shake the hand of a man who has been awarded the Medal of Honor."

He looked at Red for the first time and said with a frown, "Try to stay out of trouble, Mister Carter, and no more fights in the high school gym unless you'd like to spend some time in the county jail."

As we followed the directions given to us by the Chief, I tried to imagine how successful this might have been without the medal. My sense of it was that it was Fort Bragg all over again. If we had shown up here as private citizens wanting information to ease the mind of LaBelle Blue, I suspect we would have been told to mind our own private business and leave public business to them.

When we arrived at Lieutenant Cabot's desk, another detective was there with him. He introduced us to Sergeant Winter. They began immediately to brief us on what they knew about the murder.

The Blue girl was found on the fifteenth of February by a railway worker doing a routine inspection. Her body was located near a railroad trestle crossing Slippery Rock Creek and near also to a cabin belonging to Lana Blue. Her skull was crushed by multiple blows to her face with an iron bar found at the scene.

The body may have been seen by a man named Cotton Jimson, known around town as Doll Baby. Carriage tracks were seen near the body, and Doll Baby was known to push a baby carriage full of junk. It was difficult to get information from him because of his brain condition.

At this point, I interrupted Sergeant Winter, "I knew this man long ago, Sergeant."

"You probably don't realize how far gone he is," Sergeant Winter said. "He's been at Dix Hill for extended periods. But their findings are always the same. He's nuts but harmless. Let's put him back on the street."

After Winter had finished his recital, I asked about their opinion of Sergeant Boyd. They said they accepted the army's statement that Boyd was not implicated in the murder.

Addressing Lieutenant Cabot, "I only have two items left. First, did you ever talk with Marla Brown?"

Lieutenant Cabot told me they hadn't located her. They had tried her employer, a Mister Schwab, the owner of a bakery where both girls worked. He said she'd left his employ."

The Lieutenant wrote on a piece of paper and handed it to me, saying, "Here is the address and telephone number of the bakery, if you'd like to talk to Schwab yourself."

I told him that the only thing left was to arrange to pick up Lana's remains.

"Her family is very interested in going ahead with a funeral as soon as possible," I said.

Lieutenant Cabot said, "The Mayor asked us to present a complete report to you. We expected this subject to come up, but I regret to have to tell you that we were unable to locate Lana's body."

"You have records of her admission and identification by Mose Blue, right?"

"Somehow, these records have been misplaced." Lieutenant Cabot seemed truly distressed at having to give me this news.

"How long do they hold a body if there is no family to claim it?"

Lieutenant Cabot hesitated a moment before answering. "The answer to your question is thirty days, but that answer does not apply to this case, since no records were found of her body ever being with the Medical Examiner in the first place."

"Have you found anything at all?"

"There is a report by Sergeant Reddy that he went out to see the body of a young Negro woman, found by the railroad tracks by a rail inspector, who stated that he believed it to be the body of Lana Blue, a woman he knew as the daughter of Mose Blue. The report says that he went to the scene and examined the body and scoured the scene for evidence. He states he had the body brought in."

"What do you make of that?"

A uniformed policemen came in and handed a note to Lieutenant Cabot. He read it and told the policemen, "Yeah, tell him to come in." Turning to me, he said, "Here is someone you need to talk to. Sergeant Reddy. He's the man who wrote the report we were just talking about."

Parker Reddy, my friend Powell's brother, came into the room. Just as the Lieutenant was going to introduce us, Parker waved him off.

"I know this man, Lieutenant. He was a friend of my brother, Powell, long before the war."

He turned toward me, saying "Holly." He didn't offer to shake my hand. He was standing just inside the office door, about ten feet away from where I was sitting. He also made eye-contact with Red and gave him a nod.

I said, addressing Parker, "I guess the one fact we haven't uncovered is the location of Lana's body. Her relatives want to give her a funeral and burial."

"I have a question of my own. Why are you here? Somehow, I can't help asking myself that question." As he said this, Parker took two or three small steps toward me, cutting the distance between us to about six feet.

"I believe I've answered that already. To help a friend."

"I see. You came here to interrogate the police for your coon friends. Is that what you mean?"

Parker stepped closer to me. He was now about four feet away. I began to have the choking sensation I had around Peg at the boardinghouse.

Here was a guy, at least six feet tall and two hundred pounds, someone who may have been unhappy about the way I failed to take care of his brother. In my better days, he outweighed me by forty pounds and was at least four inches taller than me. Now, he outweighed me by at least seventy pounds. I guessed he often used his size to intimidate prisoners. I could see that would work.

"Listen, Parker, your brother was killed by the Japs. We had thousands of casualties, and Powell was one of them."

My hands were starting to tremble. If he pushed me, I might lash out at him and end up in jail.

Parker moved another two steps toward me.

"Sergeant Holly Rollins, a man who moved mud around for a living before the war, who now thinks, being a big hero and all, that he can come in here and make us jump to his orders."

He took the final step to tower over me from about a foot away. My nerves were drawn to the breaking point. With every fiber I wanted to attack him, to drive a bayonet down his throat. I wanted to see his blood run until he bled dry like a pig in a slaughter house.

Together with those feelings though, guilt had me by the throat, guilt I had not experienced before, guilt over my failure to take care of Powell.

Then, Red, who had been sitting quietly, avoiding attention, pushed past Parker, effectively moving him away from me.

Red said, "We're not going to learn anything more here. Let's go, Sergeant Rollins."

With that, he grabbed my arm and helped me get to my feet. We left Lieutenant Cabot's office. As we walked down the corridor, I heard Parker saying to the others, "Some hero. I bet it was my brother killed all those Japs, and this jerk took credit for it after my brother was killed."

I didn't want anyone looking upon me as a hero. I had seen Chesty Puller and other genuine heroes on Guadalcanal. I didn't belong in their company. Of course, I didn't want them to think I was a rat. But at the moment I was too shaken to worry about it.

This intense session at the police station had lasted more than an hour and left me exhausted. When we got to the street, I told Red I had to go home to rest.

He thought that was a good idea and suggested that we meet for breakfast in the morning to discuss this visit and figure out what to do next.

I went home to bed to a painful and restless night. I kept thinking about Powell when awake and dreaming about him when asleep. I kept remembering moments, here and there, from the night Powell died. For the first time since that night, I began to doubt my memories of what happened. Not that Parker was right, but maybe he wasn't completely wrong either.

§

The next morning, Ida and Red made a consolation visit to the diner on Whitaker Mill Road, the place where I about bit Buck's head off for his inappropriate language. Buck's attitude was nothing compared to Parker Reddy.

It was a very quiet meal. Obviously, Red had told Ida about the events at the police station.

When we were finishing our coffee, I mentioned that I was thinking of talking to Schwab at the bakery to see if he could tell us how to find Marla. Red's response was to continue to look down at the tabletop, chewing his lip. Ida sat quietly munching her salad for several minutes before speaking and then said only that I should first find out whether anyone at the bakery was connected somehow to Lana, apart from work.

Back at the house after breakfast, I considered my options: (a) Should I attempt to pat Joe, the wild cat? Or, (b) should I ignore the possibility that Ida was right and call Schwab? I could meet him at the Hall of Pool, near the bakery, and yet a place where we could talk without being observed by his employees. Clearly, Schwab was a safer choice than Joe.

When I told Schwab I wanted to ask him about Lana Blue and Marla Brown, he said, "Zo?" He agreed to meet later during the bakery's noon break.

The door was standing open when I arrived at 11:30 with nobody, not even Bad Dad, inside. I grabbed a tray of balls and took them to the back table to work on my game.

For the next thirty minutes I chased a cue ball around the table for the exercise while keeping an eye on the door. Two men came in soon after I did and took the front table. One of them was called Jesse and, although I couldn't remember the other one's name, I did remember they were both trouble makers.

Most people come to Dad's to practice or to gamble, and a few come just to drink. Everything they did was done with booze in hand and often followed by trouble and brawling.

Dad still hadn't shown up.

It was beginning to appear I might have to call in a real estate agent to take the place over when in walked Bad Dad, arm in arm with Red Carter, both seemed ready to burst into a barbershop quartet piece, like *Take Me Out to the Ball Game*. They were bad drunk.

Red noticed me at the back table and came on back there. The advantage to him in his present condition, given it was the show table, was a row of high chairs against the back wall. Red climbed up in one of these and appeared to go immediately to sleep.

57

A few minutes later, Herr Schwab came in out of the bright sunshine and stood blinking in the doorway, beginning a whole new category of people coming through that door, those who had no idea why they were in a pool room or what it was all about. He was young and looked physically fit, making me wonder why I had expected him to be fifty and fat.

I dropped my stick on the table and started toward the front of the hall. Before I was near enough to greet him without raising my voice, he had walked over to Jesse's table, stopped beside it, and stood for a moment looking down at the felt as intently as he might study a pastry tray. Then, impulsively as it seemed to me, he leaned over the table and began to rub the cloth with both his hands spread wide on the felt. Jesse, who in that moment was lining up a shot with his chin almost touching the cue stick, was completely still. His friend, leaning against the wall, was frozen in the posture of a Lucky Strike billboard, staring at the table with a blank expression and a cigarette poised two inches from his lips.

If Herr Schwab had smashed a bottle against the table, they would have immediately jumped him. But something about what he was doing took them so much by surprise that they were locked in this state of immobility. Then, as if it wasn't enough that he was blocking Jesse's shot, Herr Schwab reached over and picked up the ball Jesse was shooting at. Who knows, Jesse may have been about to move again and picking up that ball may have given him a new fixation to deal with. In any case, I looked at the pair of them, Jesse and his friend, and knew I had to rush Herr Schwab out of there while they were still immobilized.

I grabbed his arm just as he restored the ball to its place on the table and said, "Let's sit outside." But I was a bit too slow and too late. Over Herr Schwab's shoulder I saw Jesse's friend starting to come off the wall, and I had to assume for my own safety that Jesse, behind me, was also answering roll call. The unseen Jesse was the one I was going to have to deal with first, leaving Schwab to take care of himself.

Then, out of the corner of my eye, I saw a flash coming down the far wall not making a sound and running like the old days. The friend's shoulders had hardly left the wall when Flash Gordon made a perfect tackle, hitting the friend's mid-section and driving him ten feet along the floor. Unfortunately for the friend, his head made the sound a ripe melon does when you give it a good thump. As I finally managed to get turned around to deal with Jesse, I saw him from the rear as he scurried out the door. He wasn't running from me. I was sure he wanted no part of Red Carter.

Bad Dad may have had even more to drink than Red. He said, without leaving his chair, "Don't worry about Chas, he took a sleep in that same spot two weeks ago."

I dragged Herr Schwab out onto the sidewalk, parked him in a chair and sat down opposite him. Red went out a window, maybe. I never saw him come outside, though I was facing the door during my conversation with Herr Schwab, and he wasn't inside when I checked later.

Nothing about this experience seemed to have perturbed the baker, including me pulling him outside. He sat there innocently peering around, checking out the traffic and the people walking by. I waited to see if he would have a comment on what had happened, but he didn't say anything.

What the hell, I could. "How do you happen to live here in Raleigh, Herr Schwab?"

"Not live, stay until finish of war. Go back."

"To Vienna, right?"

"Ja, Vienna. Why to ask, pleez?"

I couldn't figure why I wanted to know about the Herr. I couldn't believe I could learn anything from him as unaware as he was, to the point of making me wonder how he could even get across town alive. But I did want to make sure he didn't know anything that I needed to know.

I asked him, "How did you get here? I mean, with the war on and non-military travel impossible, how did you get here?"

"When Nazis to Vienna come, I am bring Mother to Italy and am take family name, so to become Private Caruso in Italian army in Africa. One day see road sign, Cairo thirty kilometres. Leave tank. Walk to Cairo where are British.

"You were with an Italian tank battalion?"

He nodded his headed slightly.

"Serving with Rommel?"

"One year."

It struck me that the British must have had a problem with him strolling in from the desert after serving with Rommel. "When you got to Cairo, what did the British say about you fighting for the Jerries?"

This time, the Herr didn't answer right away. He sat with a bitter expression on his face, once again studying the neighborhood. After one or two minutes, he said, "Father Jew. Is why Italy go, from Nazi hide. To British Tommy I say all. He say me, 'Good job'."

"What do the people here say?"

"Say nothing." Herr Schwab was back to his out-of-focus expression.

"Tell me about Lana Blue," I asked. "What kind of an employee was she?"

"No good. Late to work drunk coming."

"Do you remember when she stopped coming?"

"Not remember, bring."

With that, he reached into his jacket pocket, pulled out an envelope and handed it over to me. I pulled two sheets of papers from the envelope and looked over the top sheet. It was like a page from the calendar for the month of February, blocked off into weeks with a small square for each day. Someone, perhaps a timekeeper, had written into some of these. The last entry was in the block for the eleventh: 8:00 - 6:00. This was just a few days before her death. At the bottom of the page was Lana's name and a rural route-number address.

The second sheet was similar to the first and showed a final entry on the thirteenth, with the name Marla Brown and a street address.

"Thank you, Herr Schwab, this is just what I needed. Tell me, why did you not get rid of her before, if she was such a bad employee?"

"Good Shepherd take care of black peoples. Like children."

It seemed it hadn't taken the Good Herr long to pick up our vices. I said to him, "I'm surprised to hear you, a Jew, talking like a racist."

"Racist, no. Fascist, like Mussolini."

This remark made it seem so obvious he was a spy that he couldn't possibly be one. But my attitude toward him was shifting from thinking him out of touch to believing that he was using camouflage like a sniper.

"So, you're a Fascist Jew who served with Rommel in Africa. Do you own a shortwave radio, Herr Schwab? Should I call the FBI and turn you in as a Fifth Column spy?

"No, no. All wrong. No spy. Catholic."

In my confusion over his answers, I found myself wondering if Mussolini was also a Catholic. Could be.

Then, he continued with, "Ask Priest at Church of Good Shepherd."

A spark of light came on, and I tried to fan it a little brighter. "Wait a minute, here. Are you saying that it is this church, The Good Shepherd, that takes care of black people?"

"Every suffering peoples. Church take care and send to bakery to work or eat bread."

"This priest sent Lana Blue and Marla Brown to you?"

For the first time, the Herr registered emotion, seemingly bewildered by my question, he shrugged while saying, "So I am say."

"I'd like to come over to talk with Marla."

"Marla no there, stopping to come after Lana stopping."

"And that date, the thirteenth, was her last day?"

Herr Schwab nodded his head.

"Very good and thanks for the address. I hope when the war is over you manage to dig yourself out of this deep hole you've hidden in and find your way back home."

I left Herr Schwab sitting in front of the Hall staring off into space, maybe still somewhat bewildered by our conversation. Certainly, he wasn't as dumb as he appeared, and the Katzenjammer accent went along with his other camouflage.

Before I left the Hall, I stepped inside to check on Jesse's friend Chas. I had seen a lot of trauma recently. Probably Chas had gotten through that and was now just asleep.

§

The Good Shepherd was downtown, only two blocks from Christ Episcopalian, the largest Protestant church in Raleigh. But, whereas Christ Church had a smart, well-fed appearance, the Good Shepherd was worn and patched, with a front lawn which was here weeds and dandelions and there bare soil. The door to the church was locked, and I went around toward the back. A solitary figure dressed in faded Navy dungarees was on his knees weeding a victory garden in the side yard of the rectory.

I walked up behind him and said, "Chaplain?"

"Yes," the man answered, getting to his feet and turning toward me. "You got me there."

"My second guess was the Army-Navy Surplus Store." I said. "But you had the look, or maybe the hair trim."

"Yes, I'm not surprised."

"As you can see, I prefer civvies. My name is Rollins, Sergeant, US Army. How come they're letting you go, Chaplain, when they're drafting everybody else?"

"It's not what you think. I was in China for ten years until Pearl Harbor. It took a year to get back, and I'm taking care of some things before beginning a new assignment."

"Did you put in this garden?"

"Yes, I did, Sergeant. After several years on a ship, I felt like rolling around in dirt for a change."

The Chaplain was in his mid-thirties. Young, I suppose, for a Chaplain with ten years on his arm.

"I have a couple of questions about Good Shepherd business. Are you the person to ask?"

"Follow me, Sergeant." With that, he went in the back door of the rectory, which was built with multi-colored stones. I followed him in and found myself in dim light, with an impression of wood and leather, the smell of candles and incense.

The Chaplain asked me to take a seat on the leather couch, while he got us some tea. In a few minutes he was back with a silver tray of tea and cookies.

"I've just come from a meeting with Schwab, the baker, who tells me that you sent Lana Blue and Marla Brown to him."

"I saw two young women on the drug path and thought a good job with a good man might help them. Lana was murdered before that got a chance to work out."

"They were both using drugs?"

"Both," answered the Chaplain. "I spoke several times about it with each of them. Neither of them made any effort to deny it."

I asked him if he had gotten to know them well enough to know who their friends were, or how they spent their time. He shook his head without comment. Then, I asked what, if anything, he knew about Marla's whereabouts. He told me that he knew her family, knew they were on hard times.

The Chaplain concluded with, "I last saw Marla just before the murder. She was afraid then for her safety. I think the whole family solved all its own problems, and took off up north to get in on that National Defense money."

The Chaplain and I talked on for another hour. I asked him a question I had been wondering about the whole afternoon. "When you were on that ship in China, did the crew come in contact with Chinese? I mean, or were you too far off-shore? If they did, what was their attitude toward the Chinese?"

"You'll have to define that a bit more for me, Sergeant. We had many contacts of many different kinds. Without knowing more about what you're getting at, I wouldn't know how to give you a good answer."

The Chaplain lit a pipe while I was asking this last question and took a few puffs to get it burning smoothly.

"Nothing out of the ordinary. Just, how did our people deal with them? Would you say that it was in a racist way?"

The chaplain was still having trouble with his pipe and re-lit it yet again. He said, "There were men on board who were thought to be expert in every phase of Chinese life. They decided how we dealt with the Chinese on every occasion. I would say it was the opposite of racist. I'd say it was calculated but correct."

I was uneasy about this conversation and starting to feel the whole subject was too big for me, maybe. It's hard for me to understand why I went on from there, but I did.

"Chaplain, have you counseled soldiers who have had problems after serving in combat?"

"Sure, that's certainly one of my preoccupations. Is there something you'd like to talk about, Sergeant?"

63

"Did any of them ever lose hope? I mean, lose the feeling that he was going to survive?"

"You mean to be in despair instead of hope?" he said.

"Yes, that's it."

The chaplain gave up on his pipe and put it away. "Did anyone ever tell you that being hopeless is a sin?"

"Father, in our circumstances, especially there at the beginning, everybody gave us up. Even Roosevelt thought we were lost and gave up."

"It's not about circumstance. It's about trusting in God. That failure to trust God is what makes it a sin."

Nothing about this conversation was working out for me. I had a ringing in my ears and a headache. It was time to leave.

But he had opened a brand new door. Where did they buy the drugs they were using? Could all this, including Marla's vanishing act be coming from the drug business?

§

While having breakfast the next morning, I got Red on the telephone, and we agreed to meet in the afternoon to go see Doll Baby. Meanwhile, it was a about time to put some effort into finding Lana's body. Even more than that now, I wanted some answers on this drug business.

I cranked up the A and drove across town to visit Mose at his store. Maybe he did know more than he realized. Then again, maybe he knew more than we realized.

Upon arriving at the store, I found Mose behind the counter and didn't waste any time, "I've come to ask you to help me find Lana's body. Also, I want to find out how she spent her time? Were there any other men around, besides Boyd I mean?"

"How come you bringing this here to me? I already told Granbelle I don't know nothing."

"She wants it done, Mose, that's all there is to it."

"Okay, Moonman, follow me." He came out from behind his counter and through a door in the corner that took us outside. We went around back and entered the barroom. There was a small table by the door and he gestured for me to sit on it, which I did.

"Knowing Granbelle, I'm sure she told you wrong. You look at Lana when she with that Marla, and you see her as hard or mean. But that's coming from Marla. She's the user and abuser, somebody you better not put too much trust in."

This sounded like my chance to jump in. "Where did she get her drugs? Did they come from you?"

"What I sell don't go in no pipe nor up your nose. It comes in a jar, and you drink it."

For the next fifteen minutes, I tried to get something more out of Mose, especially about the source of Marla's drugs. He wouldn't say for sure how he knew Marla took drugs or where she got them. However, he did know for sure that Lana was not taking drugs, but he couldn't or wouldn't give me any explanation of how he knew this, either.

Finally, I gave up and went on to the next thing. "LaBelle thought you might know something and not know you know it. I want you to tell me what happened when you went to identify Lana's body."

He looked at me as if he had doubts about where this was going but, as I soon learned, he was really thinking about something else. He began to pace around the room and, without looking at me directly, said, "I hear you know this Parker Reddy. He come in here and say to me that one night a van full of cops is gonna show up and tear my place down."

I waited for him to continue as he walked around the room, looking up at the ceiling and back down at the floor, but I don't think he was seeing them because his eyes had a blank inwardness.

"Then, he tell me that ain't why he come to see me. He said that he come himself to tell me that my judgment day was here. We got somebody down at the morgue, he said, all pegged out on a slab ready to be cut up. Know who that is?

"And, he laughed when I told him I don't know nobody down on that slab. He laughed and said how much fun he was having.

"And, then, he said that my daughter was at the morgue. He said he couldn't hardly wait for me to see how all stove-in she was."

Mose balled up his left fist and cracked the knuckles with his right hand. It made a loud noise in the quiet room. "Telling me she dead, my daughter. That's how he do."

"I know what a son-of-a-bitch he is. I'm truly sorry for all that happened to Lana, Mose, and all the pain it's caused."

I sat there in silence looking at Mose, who continued to walk back and forth in the empty room. When he finally stopped in front of me, I asked him, "Who was with him when he came to your place?"

"Just him come in here, and a law in the car by name of Brain."

"So, then you went to the Morgue, right?"

"Nope, we stop at the station, pick up that man walk the street pushing a baby carriage."

"Doll Baby. You picked up Doll Baby at the station?"

"Yep, standing in front."

"Then you went to the Morgue, right?"

"That's right."

"So, what happened? He asked you to identify Lana's body?"

"No, he didn't say nothing."

"And you identified Lana's body."

"Yes."

"Did they ask Doll Baby?"

"No, they didn't ask him. He didn't say nothing 'til later. On the way back in the car, he started to say *muddy muddy*."

"Tell me, Mose, did you ever talk to anyone here about Lana, how she died or about going down to see her body?"

Mose didn't say anything. I waited, but he didn't answer.

I asked him again, "Did you tell anybody about Lana? Leroy, for example, did you talk to him about Lana?"

"I ain't talk to nobody." Mose said, speaking softly. "About Lana, nobody."

I heard the compassion for his daughter that had been there all along without my noticing it.

Now, it was time to find a new approach. "Mose, I want you to tell me every word that Parker said, either to you or anyone. Okay?"

"Okay."

"Say anything to Brain?"

"All he say is 'Let's go' a couple of times."

"To Doll Baby, say anything?"

"No."

"To you?"

"No, he just pulled back the sheet."

I was running out of room, fast. "At the Morgue. Did he speak to anybody?"

"When we come in, he say a big number. Something like five hundert. When we leave, he step inside someplace and I hear him say, 'Same as last time'."

"'Same as last time', did I say that right?"

"That's right."

"Mose, what you heard then, did you have any idea at the time what he was talking about."

"No idea." Mose said.

"One other thing before I leave. Where is Jerome?"

"Same place he's been for years, in Salem. He's known as Reverend Bountiful."

"I'd like to call him," I said. "Do you have a telephone number for him, Mose?"

"Can't call there. They're like the Mennonites. No telephones, no machines," said Mose. "But, tomorrow is Saturday. If you go there Sunday, you'll find him on a hill just outside Salem preaching The Sermon on the Mount."

"You mean, he preaches about the one in the Bible?"

"He's been preaching about that for years. He says he's never going to run out of things to say about it."

"Why didn't you tell LaBelle?"

"Granbelle blame me for everything. If I told her that, she'd a blamed me for Jerome, too."

§

Red and I left town following railroad tracks that headed north-east from the city limits. The tracks emerged from a railroad yard that extended from near the city center all the way to the edge of town. At that point, the yard went from being five or six blocks wide to the width of a single track.

As we walked along the track, I told Red what I had found out since I had last seen him. He jumped right on Parker's statement at the Morgue.

"So you think that when Parker told the attendant, *Same as last time*, that was telling him to get rid of the body, something that had happened before?"

"I'll admit that we don't yet know exactly what Parker meant. How could they get rid of a body, anyway?"

Red walked in silence for five minutes. "I don't see how we know anything more than we did before."

"We need Parker to tell us what it all means."

"Holly, we'll never get anything out of Parker."

"Maybe, then, from Doll Baby."

We left the track just before the Slippery Rock trestle. We took a trail that came over a ridge and down into a valley formed by the creek. The woods around had been clear-cut within the past twenty years. It was all brush and stunted pine trees cluttering up the forest on both sides of the trail.

When we got to the creek a few minutes later, I was surprised to see it was the size of a river, more than fifty feet wide. The trail crossed the creek over rocks covered with black slime and patches of moss. It wasn't easy to get across.

We continued onward and soon saw a rock shelter about fifty feet from the creek. There were no trees by it. The shelter was built where the creek had taken a shorter path through a bend, leaving dry rocks that were easy to pile up to form the walls of the shelter.

"That's Cotton's place," said Red. "Lana's place is easy from here. It's just half a mile down the creek, about a hundred yards before you get to the railroad trestle."

We climbed the rest of the way down to Doll Baby's hideout. It was built in the shape of an igloo, with a crawl-way entrance protected by a suspended piece of leather.

I called Cotton's name a few times, but there was no answer. In front of his stone shelter was a baby carriage with two dolls on top of who knows what collection of useless trash. The dolls had blonde hair with huge, blue eyes and rosy cheeks.

Red said, "We can go on to Lana's and try again on the way back."

I was standing looking over the shelter, not really looking at anything, thinking about what we should do next. Then, I realized that I was looking at someone who was looking back at me. There was Cotton, sitting on a kind of throne-like stone that was about fifty feet behind and above the cabin. He was watching us invade his kingdom through age-darkened goggles attached to an old, leather aviator's cap he was wearing. The way he was perched on his throne, leaning forward and peering through those large goggles, reminded me of a praying mantis.

"Cotton," I yelled. "It's Holly Rollins. Remember me?"

Cotton didn't look away and didn't respond.

"I've come to ask you about the dead body you found, about Lana Blue."

"Muddy," Cotton shouted.

Cotton's syphilis must have perforated his brain until it was like old lace. Still, maybe I could keep him talking.

There was a steep path above the cabin leading up to Cotton's throne. When I came up near the throne, I said, "Lana Blue!"

"Lana," answered Cotton. Then, a crafty smile slipped over his face. "Lana."

"Do you remember finding Lana Blue? She was dead. Do you remember that, Cotton?"

"Muddy," muttered Cotton still sporting his odd smile.

I decided to try a fifth-grade approach. "I whipped your ASS!" I yelled in his face. "Remember I whipped your ass?"

"You stink!" said Cotton. The smile was gone and Cotton now had a defiant expression on his face.

"You ate grasshoppers," I accused him. "You stuffed them in your mouth and ate them alive."

"Praise the Lord and pass the ammunition," Cotton replied.

"I love Lana Blue! You stay away from Lana!" I pretended to threaten him.

Cotton's face had, by now, become a study with all his recent emotions colliding there. Despite the blankness of his spongy brain, his defiance and craftiness came through.

"Muddy Muddy," he chanted.

I looked back down the hill and saw Red's face looking over the top of the cabin. I shrugged.

"Lana Lana, where?" I asked Cotton. "Lana Lana, where?" I repeated, hoping to tune into his private language.

"Muddy Muddy." Cotton chanted.

"Lana gone?" I yelled at Cotton from a distance of only about five feet.

"You stink!" Cotton pulled his cap down over his ears, buckled the chin strap, folded his arms over his chest and lowered his chin onto his arms. The royal séance was at an end. The king needed his snooze. I took a final look at Cotton's goggles. No use going on.

As soon as I rejoined Red in front of the cabin, he asked, "What happened? Did you learn anything?"

"Yeah. Cotton knows something, but can't remember what. Even if he could remember, he wouldn't be able to tell us."

The rest of our visit to Slippery Rock Creek was spent looking over Lana's cabin. Neither of us had any idea of what to look for. Unlike Cotton's makeshift affair, Lana's was a well-built fisherman's cabin. On a shelf sixty feet from the creek and twenty feet higher, it wasn't as likely as Cotton's igloo to be swept away when the creek rose.

Inside, it had two beds with soft mattresses, wooden furniture, pillows on the chairs, and a red and white cloth tablecloth on the kitchen table. The only defect lay in the fact that all this sat on a dirt and sand floor.

"Just think, a murder took place here." Red said.

His voice had a note of superstitious awe.

"Watch out your imagination doesn't get too fired up, Red."

Red seemed shaken. "How could a murder happen here in such an ordinary place? Someone deliberately killed a young woman here."

"Red, she wasn't murdered here, not in this cabin, if that's what's giving you the willies. She was murdered out by the tracks and we passed the spot without even knowing it."

"You know, you're right. I could see blood spattered on the walls of the cabin, everywhere I looked."

We left a few minutes later and walked back along the railroad tracks to town without further conversation.

My pace was beyond my capacity.

For the next few days, I rested in bed and tried to get ready for the ordeal of the parade and reception. During that time, I felt some discomfort from the malaria, but the clockwork attacks seemed to be over, at least for now.

§

I needed to get some air, and I challenged Mickey to a match at Bad Dad's, with the three of us walking across town, Buck coming as a witness.

When we arrived, we found a few of the regulars lounging out front in wicker chairs. We had just walked four quick miles in warm weather and needed some liquid. Dad had beers brought out from the bowling alley next door. We were told that Red was in the middle of telling a story about our visit to Lana's cabin.

He said, "I'll admit I had a really strange feeling. I never saw a murder or a place where one happened. When I looked around poor Lana's stone shelter, I saw blood on the walls and floor. I felt like I was in a *Dracula* movie. Then, the old Sarge here ruined the whole thing. He said she wasn't killed there. As soon as he said that, Dracula went away."

Stacey snorted and said to Mickey, "I can't imagine a mutt like him acting like some redneck's widow."

Mickey added, "Who needed a whiff of smelling salts."

Looking at Stacey, Red replied, "I'm looking at a man with a neck banded like a mallard duck talking about rednecks. Just shows that he ain't got no woman at home and no mirror."

"You know," Stacey said, this time directly to Red, "I was playing with you before. I might have to throw a big fist your way."

Red said, "In a club fight, when someone does that, the other fellow butts it with the front of his skull and busts the knuckles."

Stacey turned to me and hurried onto a new subject, "You say you saw that crazy man, Doll Baby?"

Buck put his beer down on the sidewalk, "Why'd you go see him?"

I answered that one. "Mose said that Doll Baby was questioned by the police. I thought that if he knew something, he might tell me because I knew him from grade school."

"What did you find out?" asked Mickey.

"That he likes to wear an aviator's cap with goggles." I said that with finality and ended the conversation.

A few minutes later we went in to play our challenge match and played even for awhile with Buck sitting there on one of those high stools watching us. Mickey was a game up on me after three, but I was winning the fourth game. Then, Mickey settled into that mood of hers and started swishing around the table faster and faster, slamming balls into the pockets without even seeming to pay attention to what she was doing. She ran the table in under a minute and won our bet.

That made her up two games and left me almost out of ready cash. But, after paying what I'd lost, I said, "How about one more game?" I was too angry to stop.

She agreed. Since we played winner breaks, she broke and, unfortunately for me, picked up right where she left off. She made two balls on the break and resumed swishing around.

I was standing next to Buck, unable to help myself. He smirked down at me and said, "Mickey's a natural and don't even know it. She's sure slamming the hook into you, Sucker."

I understood what he meant and knew he was right, and that only made it worse. Mickey ran the table from the break and won the bet without me getting even a single shot. I paid off my bet, and Mickey went home. Buck and I sat out front in the wicker chairs, and he began telling me a story about Mickey, about their high school days in Boone, where they grew up. I didn't really want to hear a story about Mickey at the moment and was only half listening to him.

He said she was rail thin in the ninth grade. That's when she first got her bangs-like-a-bowl haircut. The next day she went to school with a bit of white lace pinned to the top of her head.

Buck told me that Chester said, "You got a shape like a stick. If you dyed your hair blue, you'd look like an Ohio match."

Maybe the story was funny, but I was too angry to laugh at it. I would have given anything if I could have beaten her when she was in that spell of hers.

Then, I noticed what he had said, "You're not talking about Chester Carmichael, are you?"

"Sure I am. I told you before that we were old friends. In fact, he was engaged to Mickey after high school until we had that big bust up."

"I guess I didn't realize that until now. So, she's over it, is she?"

"Doubt that," said Buck.

§

On Saturday morning, a limousine came to pick us up. Buck and Mickey came along and, after we had stopped to pick up LaBelle, we went to meet Mayor Battle Washburn.

The Mayor's mansion was a block on the other side of Capitol Square, a three-story stone building. As we exited the limousine, the Mayor came down the stairs as light on his feet as Ginger Rogers. "Welcome, Sergeant, welcome. Introduce your guests, please."

"Mayor Washburn, I'd like you to meet LaBelle Blue, the person I spoke to you about. And these other friends of mine are Mickey and Buck Rains, who recently moved here from Asheville. They owned a boardinghouse there, called The Dollar, where I used to live."

The Mayor shook hands all around, saying we had time only for the five minute tour, if we were interested. Of course we were. It turned out the short tour covered only the downstairs corridor, a study, a large dining room. To my surprise, LaBelle made comments as we strolled around. Looking at a trophy case in the corridor celebrating the Raleigh Police Department, for example, she commented, "Would be much more impressive, Mister Mayor, if the silver was polished, on Sundays maybe."

"Why do you say that?" asked Mayor Bats.

"Often the people are out on Sunday and other work can be done when the staff doesn't have to look after them."

Buck stepped up beside the Mayor, saying, "I'm glad to make your acquaintance, Mister Mayor. Mic and me's trying to make our way now we've come back to Raleigh. That boardinghouse burned down that Holly was talking about, and we lost our stake. Our insurance wasn't no good on account of it being arson."

"Good Heavens, Mister Rains, arson. How can I help?"

"I was thinking maybe could I get some kind of license to do something new here in Raleigh?"

"What kind of license, Mister Buck?"

"I'll let you know, soon as I figure it out, Mister Mayor."

At the end of the hallway was the Mayor's dining room, and we went in to have lunch with His Honor. By the time we had finished lunch, the conversation had slowed down and the Mayor asked me if I knew of any amusing stories about the war.

When we each had our coffee, I told this story.

"One time our Captain's tent was set up in a spot near the bodies of a couple of Japanese, and the Captain couldn't sleep for the bad odor. The next day, he told me to have them buried. I came back to his tent later and told the Captain that nobody wanted to touch them. "Captain, we don't know anything about these bodies. What if they're booby-trapped?"

"Okay, I get it. Take a patrol and go bring in at least two prisoners."

When we came back a few hours later with two prisoners, the Captain came out of the tent with a translator and with a .45 caliber automatic in his hand.

The two prisoners were right in front of him. He pointed to the one on his left and asked the translator to tell him to bury the bodies. When asked by the translator, the prisoner refused.

The Captain shot the man right in the sternum and the heavy slug knocked him back a few feet and dead on the ground.

The Captain turned to the second Japanese prisoner and stood looking at him. Before he even had a chance to ask, the man picked up the shovel and went over to bury the bodies."

I had been watching the Mayor as I told him my story, but I couldn't get a reading on him.

He said to me, "You think this story is funny?"

"What I thought was funny about it was the way the Captain figured it out in advance. He said to bring at least two."

The Mayor said to me, "Sergeant, maybe you shouldn't go back. You may have already been out there too long."

§

LaBelle and I got back into the limousine, this time with the Mayor only. Mickey and Buck were put in one right behind ours. We had a black chauffeur and LaBelle was sitting next to him. But I had a little surprise for Mayor Bats.

We drove to where the parade was forming up beside the Capitol Building on Edenton Street and took our place in line behind the North Carolina State College band, with its red uniforms and white epaulets. The Mayor informed us that the High School and City Bands would also be coming, along with drum and bugle corps from Camp Lejeune and Fort Bragg.

At the appointed hour, two o'clock exactly, the bands started to play and the limousines began to inch forward. We were doing only about a mile an hour. The open-top limo had a jump seat in front of where I was seated, directly behind LaBelle. Next to the jump seat was a metal plate in the floor with a rough surface, and there was a handrail along the back of the seat and along the window. I stood up on that plate, reached over the seat and took LaBelle's right hand and placed it in my left. I turned to wave to the crowd, not sure whether they could see we were holding hands. One person, who obviously did notice was the Mayor. This was his surprise, a bit of cheating on my deal. The Mayor had disapproval on his face for a moment, then he shrugged. All was forgiven.

It took us twenty minutes just to get around Capitol Square. As we turned onto Fayetteville Street from Morgan, we could see the length of the street to the auditorium at the other end. The sidewalk on both sides was jammed with people, spilling out onto the street, leaving about thirty feet in the middle for the bands and vehicles to pass. The Mayor had asked downtown businesses to close at 2 o'clock, and they had. In the final ordering of the parade, the drum and buglers were in the lead followed by a couple of limousines, then our limousine with LaBelle, the Mayor, and myself. The school bands brought up the rear.

As our open-top limousine passed along Fayetteville Street, people were almost hysterically shouting and holding up their fingers in Churchill's 'V' for victory.

75

I yelled at the Mayor, "There should have been a float in the parade for the First Marine Division."

He nodded and shrugged.

Bats Washburn was a real Southern politician, who could eat chittlins for lunch in the country, have tea with the Ladies' Auxiliary in the afternoon, and share a jug of liquor in the evening at the VFW. He stood up and cheered, sat down and waved, shook hands and touched babies.

It may have taken a couple of hours to get to the auditorium. I have no idea. When it was over, I was again worn out.

The Mayor told his driver to go around to the back. There we all got out and went in. The place was jammed. I looked at the Mayor and found out that he, too, had a surprise prepared. He pointed to a table skirted with red, white and blue bunting like a place fixed up for the President. In front of the table was a line a block long, ranging all the way back to the front doors and around the side wall.

"Sergeant, I believe this is your place."

Mayor Bats gestured toward a chair behind the table.

"Yes?" I didn't understand what he was getting at.

"Break a leg, as we used to say in my vaudeville days."

"You were in vaudeville? That's easy to imagine, since you always seem to be on stage."

"Yes, but it wasn't vaudeville, a bit too glamorous for what I did. If I tell you, don't tell anybody else. If you do, our deal is off. I might even have to have you killed."

"Come clean, Bats, what was it?"

"I was a comic in the burlesque. I had a tinny voice with a lisp and a partner named Storker."

"What was your stage name?"

"Death! If ever you betray me. I'll even kill your whole family. My name was Stinkypee. Storker used to chase me with a big bat with holes in it. You'd have to have seen our act to believe it was funny. But it was. Stinkypee and Storker."

"Stinkypee and Storker."

"Remember, death to your whole family!"

"I can see people are holding tickets. How much did you charge them?"

"Two dollars. That's all. Two dollars. I need that money for the upcoming election. I've got serious competition from someone I used to know in burlesque."

"It wouldn't happen to be the guy who used to beat you with a bat?" I thought of this as a joke when I said it, but then I heard the Mayor's reply.

"That would be a helluva coincidence—the dirty rat."

"Okay, Mayor Bats, I get the message." I sat down to sign autographs, wanting to help Stinkypee, but beginning to feel that I was surrounded by grifters.

§

My hand and arm were aching and the line was almost gone when Parker showed. He stopped at the end of the table and stood there, holding up a ticket and looking it over.

"Aren't you afraid the truth will come out?" He put a sneer in his voice, still staring at the ticket.

"I know lots of truths. Which one do you want?"

The Mayor, Mickey and Buck, LaBelle and Mose, and a number of other citizens were watching, not sure what was going on.

"You weren't the real hero that day, were you?"

"Without a doubt, it was your brother. It cost him his life, didn't it?"

"Don't be cute with me, you little shit. What really happened that night?"

"A grenade flew right by my face and landed behind me. Powell picked it up. When it went off, he took most of the shrapnel. I got some in my back."

Parker started to make his move on me again, stepping toward me as he said, "Yeah, the only problem with your story is that there were no witnesses."

I decided to cancel his ticket. I got up and walked toward him until I was looking right into his kisser and said, "Wrong! A Medal of Honor application has to be fully documented. The whole scene was studied and thoroughly described the following day by a committee of officers. Their documents are on file in Washington."

"You're a liar."

"Wrong, again, Parker. Whatever the medal candidate says is not counted for much in the process. The application is backed up with scientific evidence showing what really happened."

"You little son-of-a-bitch, you killed my brother yourself just to get that medal."

Mayor Bats erupted. "Sergeant Reddy, in case you're confused, this is MY reception. It was not arranged by Sergeant Rollins. So, you are coming in here disrupting the living hell out of MY reception. Get out. In the morning, I'll see you in the Chief's office. He'll let you know the time. Be prepared to spend time at the coast surf fishing."

A few minutes later, autograph signing behind me, I went straight to Buck and Mickey's house. When they dropped me, the Mayor yelled, "Good luck, Sergeant Rollins, give 'em hell when you go back!"

That evening, I sat on the edge of the bed, thinking. Memories were coming to the surface. It felt as though the struggle was theirs. They wanted to live. They wanted me to see their faces. Suddenly, I began having flashbacks, re-living moments of the past.

The moments were from the night Powell died. I had no memory of going to him or of helping him. I remembered leaving the gun, finding and opening ammo boxes, and grabbing belts for the gun. Finally, just before falling at last into a dreamless sleep, I had a memory of crawling over to look at Powell just after dawn had broken. He was still warm to the touch. He had lived through the long night, and I fell asleep wondering if a medic could have saved him.

I spent all day on Sunday recovering, taking only light refreshment, reading the Sunday paper's war news.

§

When I woke the next morning, I decided to take a walk. I needed the exercise. I put on my fatigues and boots and walked across town, down to the creek behind LaBelle's house. A few miles upstream, the creek passed through a forest where there was an abandoned sawmill. I walked to the old sawmill and rested a bit on the bench outside it.

On my way back to Whitaker Mill Road, I saw a familiar figure walking ahead of me. It was Red Carter. I quickened my pace to catch up with him. When I yelled his name, he turned and waited for me.

We stood on a street corner talking over recent events for a few minutes. Red changed the subject by saying, "You know, I didn't get a chance to tell you before because you went off to the hospital, but you woke up the world."

"What do you mean?"

"After Pearl Harbor the whole country was scared. But then the Marines slipped in the back door onto Guadalcanal and whipped 'em against all odds. Now, everyone is saying, we can do it. We can lick those Japs."

This praise made me feel uncomfortable. Any more of it and I'd probably start to get the shakes again.

"I've got some kind of heart rhythm thing going on," Red continued. "The medicos put me down as 4F."

I didn't know what to say to any of this and just asked him, "Would you like to go to a picture show?"

"Sure," Red replied. "I was just wandering around anyway."

We walked down to State Street and looked over two movies being offered. There was 'Bataan' with John Wayne. No, thanks. When we came to the Palace Theatre, we found a picture with Randolph Scott as Wyatt Earp. Perfect.

There were mostly farmers in the audience. Once, when Randolph Scott was riding toward a big rock where an outlaw was hiding, one of them yelled, "Watch out! He's behind the rock!" When a fight broke out in a bar room scene, three or four farmers leaped to their feet and began swinging punches in the air to help out the hero, yelling "I got 'em....I got 'em."

After the picture show, we went to an oyster bar on Jones Street to have a beer. Outside the back door was a Mount Shasta-shaped pile of oyster shells higher than the restaurant. We went in and found it quiet at this hour in the late afternoon.

Two sections of the restaurant were separated by a short hallway. Coming in the front door, you saw a small bar off the hallway to the right. The main dining section was farther down the hall. The bar had a window looking out onto the street, four stools and two tables. Red and I took one of the tables and ordered beer and a platter of oysters.

While we were waiting for the beer, I told Red, "During the motion picture, I had a brain hiccup or whatever you call it. You remember Leroy, right?"

"Your old pal from the bowling alley."

"Yeah, that's right. At Fort Bragg, I read an interview of Leroy by an Army Captain who asked Leroy if he knew Lana Blue or Marla Brown. You know what he said?"

Before he had a chance to answer our beer showed up, a pitcher with two frosted mugs.

Red said, "I'm damned thirsty." He took a couple of gulps from his mug and said, "They were his sisters by different fathers?"

'No, dammit all, Red. He said because of the colors in their names, he remembered them. Blue and Brown."

Red had a 'so-what' expression and said, "So?"

"So, he's a liar. How could he work there and not know Mose's own daughter who, on top of that, used to work there?"

The bartender brought our oyster platter, fresh and embedded in crushed ice, with cut halves of lemon and hot sauce on the side. We each helped ourselves to a couple.

Red said, "Before answering, let me tell about something you need to know. The weekend just before Lana was killed, she had a fight with Leroy. I was trying to get down there on Saturday night late. I suppose it was around two or three o'clock in the morning. As I came up to the streetlight on that corner by the college, I saw Lana and Leroy under that light hitting each other."

"Red, you sure you got that right? I mean, who it was? Hard to believe anything was going on between those two."

"I'm sure what I saw. I stood in the dark and watched them. I suppose I didn't interfere because she was winning the fight. I never saw a fight like it before. The two of them would walk around slowly with their hands down, staring at each other, neither one saying anything. Then, one of them would punch the other in the face. They would lean against each other for awhile before beginning again."

"You thought Lana was winning?"

"Twice when she hit him, he went down on his ass. She was hitting him a lot harder than he was hitting her."

"He could be the one who killed her. Let's go talk to him, beat it out of him, if we have to."

The bartender brought us another pitcher of beer.

Red said, "That sounds like my line of work." Looking out the window he added, "Here comes someone you may know."

A moment later, Sergeant Winter came into the bar, noticed us and came over to our table.

"I was looking for you today, Rollins," he said. "I've got some bad news."

"Hello, Sergeant Winter. This is Red Carter, the famous footballer."

The policeman didn't offer to shake our hands.

He said, "Better known now-a-days as the infamous boxer. 'Lo, Red. It's been a while. How're they treating you in the drunk tank?"

Winter turned back toward me. "That crazy friend of yours got himself killed."

"Who are you talking about?"

"Your friend, Cotton Jimson, The Doll Baby guy. Got himself killed and dumped on the tracks, where a train cut him in two. But he was already dead when that happened."

Maybe I'd had too much beer, already. I couldn't follow the policeman's story. "Are you saying that somebody killed Cotton by putting him down in front of a train?"

"Lieutenant Cabot said the killer probably thought the train would mess up the body too bad for us to get anything on him. Only, the doc said Cotton was dead at least an hour before the train tore him up.

"Wanna know any more, read it in today's paper, front section, back page. Good luck in the Pacific, Rollins, when you get back there."

Sergeant Winter left the bar and turned toward the dining section.

Red grabbed my elbow as I started to get up to go get a newspaper. "Hold up a second."

To the barman he said, "Got a copy of today's paper?"

Without saying a word, the man reached under the counter and handed a newspaper to Red.

Red took the paper and said, "And we'll take another pitcher."

He took the front section, folded it over to the back page, and handed it to me, saying, "Read it and tell me what it says."

I took the paper and read the article. A railroad inspector walking the tracks from the north at about 7:00 p.m. last night had found Cotton Jimson's body near the Slippery Rock trestle. It seems he was in town yesterday yelling at people on the street in that sing-song way he did sometimes. Anyway, the police arrested him for disturbing the peace and released him at about four o'clock in the afternoon. That was the gist of it.

The bartender interrupted me, putting down our next pitcher of beer.

I read through the brief story several times and couldn't find any answers. He was a harmless man. No danger to anyone, even to the person who murdered Lana Blue.

Red said, "Cotton knew something—and we just talked to him. This seems to me like too much of a coincidence."

"Let's go talk to Leroy, Red. Maybe he's got some answers for us."

§

It was full dark when we got to South Street. Red had gotten talkative after four hours of swill and kept up a stream of gab. There was no moon and staying on the road in the dark was not easy after all those pitchers of beer.

The dirt had a bit of crunch that could be heard and felt. Anyone watching would have thought we were drunk, the way we veered back and forth trying to keep on the crunchy part of the road. Maybe we really were drunk. I remember sometimes I had to hold on to Red's shirttail to keep up with him.

There were no customers when we walked into the store, and Leroy was busy closing up. He went behind the counter and asked us what we wanted.

I walked slowly up to the counter, focused on not knocking anything off the shelves, and came up in front of Leroy. My anger over Cotton's death came surging back.

"You killed Cotton Jimson." I shouted.

"What?" said Leroy.

In an even louder voice, I yelled, "Where is Marla?"

"Marla?" Leroy's eyes got wide and blank, like even the question was a shock to him. I wanted to put more pressure on him.

"What happened to Marla?" I shouted even louder than before.

Leroy came around his counter and shoved me in the chest.

He said, "I don't know nothin' about no murder. Get outta here."

I grabbed his arms and said, "You better know something."

Leroy broke loose from my grip and answered, "You ain't the police. Why you keep comin' in here?"

We were standing only a foot apart.

In a normal speaking voice, I said to him, "Here's what I'm going to do for you, Leroy. I'm going to tell my friends the Mayor and the Chief of Police that you're the killer."

Then, I pointed a finger at him and started shouting again. "You're the one who killed Lana Blue. You're the one who killed Cotton Jimson. You're the one who killed Marla Brown."

Leroy whirled and fled out the back door.

I stood there watching the door slam behind him.

Red grabbed my shoulder and turned me around. "What are you doing?" Red said.

"I'm not sure. Maybe I was hoping to scare something out of him. Did I go too far?"

Red was staring out the back door where Leroy had gone. "Have you told the police all this?"

"I don't know anything they don't know. Besides, with their crummy attitude, what would they do if I did tell them something important?"

Red opened the back door and looked out. "You shouldn't'a told Leroy what you did."

"Why not?"

"You've been away from the South too long. Telling Leroy you're going to turn him over to the police for murder's the same as telling him he's gonna get beat to death."

We went back out to the front of the store and stood in the darkness waiting for our eyes to re-adjust before walking back. Suddenly, I heard a slight noise behind me and felt a searing pain in my back. My breathing stopped and I fell to the ground as a sudden weakness took my legs out from under me.

I fell on my side with my eyes wide open but unable to breathe. In the soft light from the store, I saw Leroy with a butcher knife. 'Bap! Bap! Bap!' Red hit him three times, rapid fire, and put him down on the ground. Then, Red stood over Leroy and yelled, "You sum-bitch!"

I was choking, the same way I did in the smoke and fumes the night Buck and Mickey's boardinghouse burned down in Asheville. Then I couldn't breathe at all.

The last thing I remembered was calling out to Red, "Go get Buck and Mickey."

Chapter Three

Make sound, quick decisions.

----Combat Leader's Field Guide

Saturday   November 1, 1941

It was damn luck in 1939 that I signed up with the WPA for a Roosevelt job during the Great Depression. They looked over my license on steamrollers and sent me to a crew in western North Carolina to work highway construction jobs. I spent three years with that crew, finishing up near Asheville in 1941.

We stayed in Asheville at *The Dollar Boardinghouse*, where a dollar got you a bed and a place at the table twice a day. Also, on Saturdays, you got clean sheets and a chance to take a hot bath. *The Dollar* was a three-story, mid-nineteenth century brick house built just a few blocks from downtown by a successful merchant who outlived his heirs. The house sat abandoned for years until Buck and Mickey came along and saw that it was perfect for them. There were ten small rooms with windows on each of the second and third floors, and four large rooms on the ground floor. They restored it to livable condition, adding electric lights in all the rooms and indoor plumbing on each floor.

Buck did the maintenance around the place and took his supper with the boarders. I got to know him in the talk going on around the table. Mickey didn't eat with us because she was the cook and did a fine job of it, too. So said all of us.

Unlike the rest of the crew, I didn't spend my free time getting drunk. I shot pool at the Empire Pool Hall just four blocks away from *The Dollar*. By coincidence, Buck came often to the same place, and Mickey came now and then. I spent a lot of time with them shooting pool. Maybe that's why I was right in the middle when trouble came.

Buck was a savvy guy with hidden connections around town. If you wanted to watch Willie Mosconi in a private, big-money match, Buck could get you in. He could get last-minute tickets to anything going, such as pro tournaments in golf or billiards. Also, at any time of the day or night, Buck could get you moonshine for much less than it cost anywhere else. He often boasted about his friendship with a man who supplied booze to most of North Carolina.

When Buck shot pool, he made the cue ball look like it was trained to do things you didn't know a cue ball could do. I soon found out that he was able to train people to do surprising things as well.

I heard that Buck got his name from his habit of betting on any and every thing. He might point to a penny gum machine and say, "Bet'ch'a buck the next gumball's a red." Or, he might point to a door and say, "Bet'ch'a buck the next guy through that door is smaller'n you are."

As he was offering his bet, he'd be reaching into his shirt front pockets to haul out one of the wadded-up dollar bills he kept there. Often a couple of them fell onto the floor unnoticed. When I was around, I'd pick them up and stuff them back into his pocket.

The crew finished early that Saturday afternoon. When I got to the Empire, I saw Buck at the last table. I took a seat on a high stool, eager to see him in action. He was playing a guy wearing a worn suit, certainly no disgrace during the Depression. The way this guy tried to spruce it up with a bright tie and silvery stick-pin and the grim expression on his face, I figured him for a pissed-off shoe salesman.

Watching Buck, I saw him playing safe instead of taking an easy shot. He left the cue ball blocked in a corner. He dug into the shoe guy a little by saying, "See what you can do with that."

The shoe guy didn't get a hit on the object ball, giving Buck ball-in-hand. That meant Buck could put the cue ball wherever he wanted. Buck started toward the table, walking like he was drunk. He lurched and pitched forward, his feet scampering to catch up to his head. He ended up smacking into the table.

"Wash that step. Izza dilly," Buck said.

He put the cue ball down on the table and studied the felt like he was making a golf putt. He hiccupped and moved the cue ball a smidgeon and brushed the felt around it with a handkerchief. When he shot, he slammed the ball into a pocket. The cue ball spun in place for a few moments at the spot where it had hit the other ball, then took off, caroming off the cushion and stopped, lined up for a shot on the next ball. Perfection.

Again, instead of making this easy shot, Buck did another safe play and left shoe guy nothing to work with. Dropping the stagger, he walked to his chair saying, with scorn in his voice, "Now, see what you can do with that, moron." The words were not slurred.

I felt sorry for shoe guy. Not only was Buck taking his money, he was slamming him with these top-notch insults. It didn't seem fair. Shoe guy moved toward the table, expression more than grim, his face bright red, and the hand holding his cue stick shaking. He stood beside the table for two minutes. I believe he was trying to get himself calmed down.

That went out the window when Buck said, "You're wasting my time. Go ahead and shoot. You're gonna miss it anyway."

The man turned toward Buck with his stick held across his body making me think he was going to hit Buck alongside the head with it. Instead, the stick hit the floor with a loud swack, and he swung a slow-moving left hook at Buck, who ducked so fast he lost his balance and fell off the stool. Shoe guy fell on top of him, and the two of them started rolling around on the floor.

I yelled 'Roscoe!"

A voice yelled back, "Get out of my way!" and passed me on the run. Did I mention Roscoe was big, if you count six foot six and two hundred and fifty pounds as big?

Roscoe grabbed shoe guy from behind by his collar and yanked him up. Holding him up on his tiptoes, Roscoe goose-walked him toward the door and told him, "Mister Schroeder, you need to go home and cool off. I'll see you again next week."

I think Roscoe's grip was cutting off the guy's windpipe. The best Mister Schroeder could manage, was "Thump oogles gug."

I suppose you learn to understand strangled talk if you make a habit of goose-walking people around. Roscoe told me later that Schroeder said, *That sounds good*."

Buck left just after Schroeder did. There were no more customers in the place. Roscoe and I went out front to have a smoke.

He told me that he had known Buck from his early years in Boone. Roscoe lived there during the time Buck and Mickey Rains were in high school.

Around Boone, Buck was known for his mischief. "There was a saying about Buck even then: 'when it's Rains, it pours'."

Roscoe went on to explain that Buck was a hustler and Schroeder one of his regular victims. "You know, Buck's got a dicey rep around town. Plus, you gotta admit he looks and sounds suspicious. That's what shows he must be a genius, because he still manages to corral suckers."

"How does he do that?"

Roscoe sat down and flattened a large hand on top of his bald head, "He gets a grip on them somehow. Then, he just takes their money, more regular than the tax collector. To me, the oddest thing is the bad habit he has of making them angry on purpose, like tonight. Still, they keep coming back."

Roscoe took a dollar from his pocket, wadded it up and threw it on the floor. He said, "Bet'ch'a buck Schroeder comes back next week and gets trimmed again."

'My ol' pappy warned me off sucker bets." I picked up the dollar and stuffed it into Roscoe's shirt pocket.

The next evening, when Buck and I were resting between games, I found out why he raked people over the way he did. It was simple; I just asked him.

"Buck, people say you've got a skill with taking money from suckers. How do you do that?"

Buck studied the ceiling, scratching under his chin, maybe deciding whether or not he wanted to share his secrets with me.

Then he said, "You put the hook to him and slam it in hard to make him mad as hell. You throw the old reversal, making him think he's gonna slam you back. And that's the whole thing. Once he's planning to make a sucker outta you, that makes one outta him."

I could see how he kept taking money from the same guys over and over again, and I was glad he never set his sights on me.

§

For the next few days, the crew worked long hours pouring cement. Then, we got an unexpected and heavy rain one morning and were given the day off. I decided on a movie, so I could rest a bit.

The newspaper listed a picture called *Stagecoach* with John Wayne. He was great in the *Three Mesquiteers*. At the theater I took a seat in the middle. I knew this as a place where you might feel a rat brush over your shoes. There were just two other people, sitting right in the center of the front row.

The show began with Paramount News. A Dave O'Brien short picture about cigarette smoking followed the news, and I was laughing at that when a man sat down in the seat next to mine. He put his elbow on the chair arm, making contact with my elbow, even pushing his arm against mine. I looked around and saw the theater was still almost empty. I tilted my head sideways to look along my nose at the man who was making the nerves in my arm twitch. He turned his head to look directly at me. Even in the darkness of the theater, I could see the square face and low forehead of a man who would always badly need a shave. The lower half of his face was whiskery blue.

He whispered, "My boss Chester is an old friend to Buck and Mickey. He's unhappy to see Buck lining up with his enemies."

"You want me to tell that to Buck, right?"

"No, I want you to give him this piece of paper. It has a telephone number where he can talk to Chester. He needs to make that call. Like I said, they're old friends."

I took the paper and said, "You think you could move to another seat? You're making me nervous."

The man stood up, but had a last word, "This message is good for today only because there's no time left. Was I you, I'd not hang around a guy who might have a big target on his chest by tomorrow."

He turned and went up the aisle. If the picture had been anything less than John Ford, I don't believe I'd have been able to watch it after that conversation. But I did watch it and forgot all about the messenger and his message until the picture was over.

Afterwards, I dropped by the Empire looking for Buck. He wasn't there. I went back to the boardinghouse and saw him sharpening the blades of his lawn mower.

I said to him, "I've got a telephone number where you can reach Chester. The guy who gave it to me said that Chester is remembering your friendship today. But not hearing from you by midnight, that's off."

Buck looked at me without speaking for a minute. Then, he asked, "What did this guy look like?"

"One of those guys who needs a shave as soon as he finishes shaving. Dark black hair and blue chin. Husky, not tall."

Buck shook his head once and said, "That was Chester Carmichael."

"You want me to leave the number on the dining room table?"

Buck nodded his head and turned back to the mower blades. I went in and put the paper under the sugar bowl.

§

We finished pouring cement by the end of that week. On Saturday, we finally got an evening free. I rushed off to the Empire, feeling a big need to have a lively evening.

The place was busy with players at every table. I saw Schroeder, the shoe guy, shooting at the last table again. Mickey was leaning against the back wall, holding a cue stick, waiting her turn to shoot against him. Buck was watching from the other side of the table. Who knows the hearts of men? It made me wonder if Schroeder wasn't really the one with a big target painted on his chest. It was starting to look lively, but I had no idea what was coming next.

Someone grabbed me from behind as I approached Buck. People scattered out of our way as I was tossed around and, then, thrown to the floor with a knee in my back and a voice in my ear shouting, "Don't move."

I figured it was Chester who was on me, and under the circumstances I took what he said as more than a suggestion. My attacker put a grip on my head and began to grind my face into the wooden floor. This was not kosher to increase the punishment without waiting to see if I would do what he asked. Then he did it again. He shifted to a choke hold around my neck and began to tighten it up. That was too much and I gave up my passive role. Twisting around, I managed to get my knees under me and lifted us both up. Just as I was ready to flop over backwards and smack him against the floor with me on top, something banged behind my ear and I went out cold.

The next thing I knew, someone was putting cold water on my face. I opened my eyes and saw Mickey looking down at me with a sponge in her hand.

"He's back." She said.

Buck's voice said, "Holly, my friend, you just met Kelly of the FBI."

I guess I was still dizzy. I answered Buck, "I know that joke. That's the one where Kelly of the FBI is really Sally of the Secret Service in disguise."

Buck helped Mickey to her feet and she was staring him in the face when she said, "Buck is the joke. He's appearing in court against a friend of ours. He goes free and Chester goes to prison. Some joke."

I asked, "What's it all about?" My head was getting something going but my feet were still numb as I started to get up.

Kelly of the FBI offered his hand to help me and said, "Sorry, Buster, I'm not paid to take chances and I didn't know your mug. Chester Carmichael is charged with racketeering because he controls the whiskey coming down from these mountains."

As soon as I was on my feet, Kelly moved into a guard position behind Buck.

I waited until he turned around and told him, "Go tell J. Edgar Hoover I'm not a practice dummy for the FBI. After that, tell yourself to go to hell."

Kelly didn't respond, but Mickey whispered to me, loud enough for everyone to hear, "Forget these thugs in suits. Let's leave them to Buck and go back to the house. We'll have some pie with ice cream."

§

I didn't realize yet that I had steamrolled the last road I would do for the WPA. Having finished the job of turning a section of dirt road into a two-lane concrete highway, we were scheduled to give the same treatment to a road near Shelby. Only somebody upstairs made the decision that I was no longer needed. That Saturday when I got my pay envelope, I was told they were giving me an extra few bucks to pay me off. The envelope had my regular week plus an extra forty dollars.

I caught one of our trucks going into town and went over to *The Dollar* to get my stuff together. My room was paid through the end of the week. Nothing was holding me back. I didn't see anyone around until I checked the kitchen. I found Mickey there cleaning the oven.

As soon as she saw me coming in, she knew something was going on. "What happened?" she asked.

"I got paid off. Gotta go back to Raleigh right away to get signed up again."

"Where will you stay while you're there?"

"I don't know, Mickey. It's been a while since I lived there."

Mickey said, "Buck and I used to run a boardinghouse there. We turned it over to friends when we left. I'll write a letter to them. Who knows, they might give you a special rate or a cheap room."

"Thanks, Mickey. Anything would help. It might be weeks before I get another Roosevelt job."

Mickey sat down and started writing a letter. I went to my room and got my stuff packed. When I came back downstairs, Mickey handed me an envelope.

"Give them this letter. And, I want you to be on the lookout for a young woman who lives there. Her name is Ida Patini. I wrote it on the back of the envelope. If she's not still there, you can find her working at a beauty parlor in the Nash Hotel on Dawson Street. I think you'll like her. She's a very spirited young lady."

A few minutes later, I said goodbye to Mickey and went out to the highway my crew had just finished, to try to hitch a ride to Hickory.

I stood by a manual gas pump on the side of the road. If anyone stopped there, I planned to ask them for a ride. It just didn't seem that anybody was going to Hickory, or even back out to their farm. The road was empty.

After about an hour, a nineteen-thirty-eight, four-door Ford sedan appeared coming from the direction of downtown Asheville. I noticed that it was a bootlegging car that was riding about ten inches too high in the rear. I poked out my thumb. When it pulled over and stopped, I got in. There were two men sitting in the back seat. The driver started to pull out onto the highway.

I said, "Thanks for the lift. Are you going as far as Hickory?" As these words were coming out of my mouth, I recognized the driver as Chester, the friendly elbow.

He said, "These are two associates of mine, Sonny, on the left, and Anders."

"Did you come looking for me?"

"Someone is watching the boardinghouse. They told me you left carrying a suitcase. When you weren't at the bus station, I thought you might ride your thumb."

"How's the trial going, Chester?"

"I figured you'd know who I am. The FBI says I'm a racketeer and then brought out fake evidence. But, we've evened things up by faking a few things on my side. I guess that's justice for you."

"How can you say you're not a racketeer, when you run booze over two states?"

"The whiskey Daniel Boone gave the Indians came from my family. It's still all family. I'm just a trucker. But, I'm not here to talk history. I want to talk about Buck."

Although we had just left Asheville, we were driving through wooded, hilly country on a road following a mountain stream. Chester pulled over by some mailboxes and cut the engine.

"Why's Buck so scared? You don't seem like Al Capone to me."

"I'm taking you back to The Dollar. You need to tell Buck that if he testifies, the mountain people will kill him."

"What should I tell him to do?"

"His only choice is not to testify. He still has family in Boone. They will die, too."

'It's kind of hard for me to believe you'd murder his family, Chester."

"Holly, you have to understand that this is not just about me. I won't order anyone to kill them, but someone will do it."

"If you're saying that you don't want that to happen, why can't you stop it?"

"Buck knows why. He grew up working these mountain stills. There's a code of silence among these moonshiners that is absolute, no exceptions."

"So, you can't stop it."

"No, I can't. But I'm not going to hide from you that I do have people working for me who will come after Buck if he testifies and leaves Asheville."

"All right, Chester. I'll go back and talk to Buck."

Chester started the car and turned back toward Asheville. We hadn't come far and were soon at The Dollar. Chester let me out a block away at four o'clock in the afternoon.

I found Buck in the kitchen with Mickey who was standing at the table chopping vegetables. Buck was sitting across from her with a cup of coffee in his hand.

I told them about my talk with Chester. They both listened without interrupting my story. When I finished, they looked at each other without saying a word.

Finally, Buck turned back to me and said, "I don't have family in Boone, anymore. My little sister moved to Lenoir two years ago. She was the last one still living there. He suckered you with that thing about his family, Holly. Chester gets a percentage on every jar sold in his territory. He says he's like a trucking company, but it's really the protection racket. To sell to the public, you got to buy from him."

Mickey said to him, "Buck, if you go through with this tomorrow, we'll both have to be out of the mountains within twenty-four hours."

"Mickey, I've been thinking about this for weeks," said Buck. "I probably know a couple of hundred of these people. Maybe, twenty of them are killers. I bet'ch'a buck most of those were ready to kill me as soon as I talked with the FBI. A handful of them would kill me just for saying their names out loud in a public place."

"So, what are you saying? You mean it doesn't matter whether you testify or not?"

"You don't get it. My name is already in their books. I needed to testify to get the FBI to go on helping me."

That didn't sound right to me. "What do you mean you needed to testify? You're not up 'til tomorrow."

"They made a change, and I testified today. I don't know why, so don't ask me."

I believe Mickey was surprised to hear this. She asked him, "Where's Kelly? Is he on the job? Looking after you still, I mean."

Buck looked down at the tabletop and said, "He figures Chester will leave me alone now that I've had my say. He said to call him if I see any suspicious characters hanging around the place."

"Is that how you see it?" said Mickey.

"Some of them would kill me just for saying their names out loud," said Buck. "I already told you that and they ain't the forgettin' and forgivin' kind."

For the next hour, I listened to them going back and forth about what they should do. Finally, I was too tired to stay up any longer, "I'm going to stay here tonight and get on the road early in the morning. Goodnight." I went to my old room and got right to sleep.

I woke up needing to exercise the plumbing, grateful it was nicely fixed up indoors. When I opened the door to leave my room, I at once sensed something was not right.

Did I have a trace memory of a loud thump? The air was clear. Wasn't it?

I went back to my room and dressed, with a growing sense of unease, but still without being able to say why. This time when I stepped back into the hallway, I felt an irritation in my nostrils, yet I couldn't identify what was causing it. I hurried down the stairs.

When I got to the ground floor, I saw Buck coming out of the kitchen. He said, "I thought I smelled something burning but there's nothing on the stove."

To my left was a wooden panel shielding a stairway. The door to the basement was at the foot of these stairs. Buck opened the panel and, as soon as that was removed, we each knew that the odor was coming from down there.

Buck went down, and I watched him from the head of the stairs. He opened the basement door and a loud whoosh brought a rush of hot gas and smoke up the stairway. Some of it got into my lungs and I choked and coughed. The exposed skin of my face and hands began at once to sting. Buck rushed back up the stairs, and I could see that his clothing was blackened and a pant leg and sleeve were aflame.

I followed him into the kitchen where he doused the flames. He shouted at me, "I'm phoning the operator. Get everybody out as they are, no time to get dressed."

I ran up the stairs to the third floor screaming "FIRE" as loud as I could, still coughing and gasping. Once on the top floor, I threw open each door, yelling "FIRE! GET OUT NOW!"

As I started down to the second floor, I saw people emerging from some of the rooms, but not all. I turned back and yelled, "EVERYONE OUT NOW!"

The stairway was full of smoke and the visibility was dropping fast.

By the time I got to the second floor, every door was open and people were already on the stairs, all of them in their night clothes. A few were carrying shoes.

There were eighteen rooms occupied that night, twenty-four people. Twenty-six if you count Buck and Mickey. All of them made it out to the street, as far as I knew. By the time we got there, we could already hear the sirens of fire trucks coming from several directions. Moments later, the street began filling up with fire trucks. Firemen were running all over the place, spreading out and joining hoses.

The fire was surging up from the basement into the house and was visible through the downstairs windows. Several firemen started in through the front door and had to turn back.

Officials from the Fire Department began to question Buck and Mickey, who were the only ones from the house still standing on the sidewalk on that side of the street. Though they were only twenty feet from me, I couldn't hear a word they said. The fire was now loud and becoming louder by the moment.

The firemen were powerless to stop the fire in The Dollar. They concentrated their effort on making sure it didn't spread through the neighborhood. It wasn't long before the flames were shooting up hundreds of feet. The spectacle resembled a New Year's bonfire when the neighbors get together in a park or vacant lot to burn Christmas trees. It was just a matter of scale. The flames from the house went many times higher into the night sky.

The fire was burned out by daybreak.

Buck and I were sitting on the curb across the street, hidden from the house by fire trucks, having a cigarette, when he started to moan. Then, he said, "Oh! No! Oh! No!" He jumped up and ran down the block and across the street. There, parked on the same side of the street as The Dollar, was a truck belonging to Buck's father. I had followed him about half-way. He ran back into the yard and up to one of the firemen.

Buck was explaining the situation when I came up behind him, telling the firemen that he feared his father might have been there, that he sometimes came in for a visit late at night, that he had a key to the backdoor and that he sat up a cot for himself in the large pantry. He usually brought a jug with him and took on enough bedtime sauce to sleep through smoke and ruckus.

There was nothing I could do. The firemen were not going to let me into the smoldering hulk of The Dollar. Fortunately for me, I had saved my belongings because they were already packed and ready to go, and I brought the suitcase with me when I came out of The Dollar.

A truck driver on his way to Greensboro picked me up. He said he was carrying furniture, but he could have been working for Chester, as far as I knew. We got into Greensboro later that morning, and I managed to get to Raleigh in the afternoon.

The address on South Street Mickey had given me was across the street from the public auditorium. I was hoping if they had a room for me, they might also feed me. Lucky for me, that's just the way it worked out. The place was run by Bob and Peg Jones, and their daughter Megan helped with making up the rooms. They put me in a room right next to the bath on the top floor, the cheapest one they had.

Peg took me up to see it and asked, "How are Mickey and Buck?"

"I'm sorry to say their place in Asheville just burned down."

"My God, was anyone hurt?"

"Yes, one person. Their father was killed. It was terrible. Buck and I got everybody else out of the house in plenty of time. But, we didn't know his father was there."

Peg wanted Mickey's address, and I gave it to her.

The next day was a Monday. I spent it waiting at the WPA office without getting to see anyone. I went back there very early on Tuesday morning and, just before noon, I sat with a clerk and made out an application. She said they would send a letter to the boardinghouse on South Street when they found something for me.

§

I went out to Fontaine Street to let LaBelle know I was back from Ashville, at least temporarily. I found her in the yard hanging wet sheets. It was a sunny day, good for business. She was focused on what she was doing and didn't notice me standing on the sidewalk, just a few feet away.

It was a pleasure to stand there quietly and watch her at work, and I enjoyed it for several minutes.

Then I said, "Tatie," and walked down the bank to where she was now looking up from her work.

"I've missed you," I said.

"I can hardly believe you're not still living next door. One day you were there and the next day you were gone."

"I had a fight with my stepmother and was dumb enough to threaten to hit her. My father threw me out into the street."

"I'm dealing with the same, turned around the other way. I threw Lana out because of her bad behavior, like her father and brother all over again."

"The Blues live up to their name."

"I met Tyler when he was a young preacher who never drank, and I thought he was a temp'rance man. Two weeks after we wed, he came home drunk, and I didn't let him come in the house. I couldn't stop him from drinking, but I didn't plan on helping him do it. He had some sober times, and we had two children, Mose and Annabethe. She died in the big influenza time.

"When Mose took on like his father by age twelve, I put them both out of the house and they built a cabin on Slippery Rock Creek. When Mose was eighteen, he fooled some woman as dumb as me, name of Sue Annie, and soon Jerome was born, and Lana a few years later.

"But Jerome took after his father and tried to make the world safe from liquor by drinking it all up. He ran off with a woman I didn't ever know. Then his and Lana's mother, poor thing, turned cokey and disappeared down a drug rat hole someplace. That's when Lana took her turn living here."

It was something to hear this story, and I said, "Tatie, I guess we're just stuck with each other. Most all the family we got left."

LaBelle said, "Come give me a hug."

After the hug, she said, "If you weren't so big now, I'd take you in my lap like I used to and sing you a lullaby, maybe that Irish one you like, *Danny Boy*."

§

Later, I walked over to Bad Dad's Hall of Pool. A block before I got there, I passed the Nash Hotel and two thoughts drifted through my brain. First, I remembered there was a soda fountain in the lobby where I should be able to get a hot dog. Second, I remembered Mickey telling me about Ida Patini. I wasn't sure what I could do about that item, but the first one sounded like what I needed.

The lobby was dim and cool after the bright and warm weather outside. The floor was tiled in black and white squares. There were huge ceiling fans with blades about twelve feet long, reminding me of the slow-turning blades of an auto-gyro airplane. The soda fountain was located along a corridor behind the front desk. I passed a tobacconist/newspaper dealer in the lobby and saw a beauty parlor down the hall.

A small, middle-aged man stood behind the soda-fountain counter, and I asked him about the help-wanted sign on the door. He said, "My name is Wode. Torry Wode. I just put that up. The young man who had that job enlisted in the Navy this morning. You can have the job if you want it."

Mister Wode spent about an hour teaching me the drinks and the layout. After that he left, and I was on my own. I could hardly believe I had this job, and I was nervous about never having served a customer before.

The first one who came in turned out to be Ida Patini, the woman Mickey told me about, though I didn't realize it was her right away. When she came in the second time, I told her about our shared connection to Mickey, and she said she was happy to hear of it. Not long afterwards, we went out on a date to a nightclub.

On the way to pick her up, I had the taxi driver stop at a gas station, and I came away with a quart jar in a plain, brown paper bag. If you wanted anything stronger than beer or wine in North Carolina, you had to bring it yourself and buy set-ups from the bar.

When we got to Ida's rented house on Jones Street, she came out onto the front porch and damned if she wasn't dressed like a bobbysoxer. She was wearing mid-calf, thick white socks folded over a couple of times until they rested just above her ankles in a three or four inch fold. She had on a white, bulky cashmere sweater and a knee-length, flared and pleated, dark brown skirt. The laces of her brown and white saddle shoes were tassels with little bells on the ends.

I asked her, "How am I going to get you into a nightclub, Ida? You look like a junior-high cheerleader."

"How would you know about school? You struck out."

"That's baseball, Ida. It's dropped out when you're talking about school." Even as I said this, I saw that Ida was someone who found ways to shut you up even when she got it wrong.

The nightclub was a restaurant on Glenwood Avenue just where you leave town heading toward Durham. It was really just a steak and potato place with a four-piece band for entertainment and a dance floor large enough for a dozen couples.

As soon as we were seated, I opened the white lightning. It smelled and tasted like kerosene. If Daniel Boone gave this stuff to the Indians, they would have taken his scalp. The best I could do with it was to mix it with the strongest-flavored sodas. I ordered a root beer for Ida and a Dr. Pepper for myself.

The musicians of the band were doing a fair job on a Benny Goodman number, as arranged by Fletcher Henderson. The clarinet player was no Benny Goodman—but who is?

In between dances, Ida told me that Mickey had shown up at the beauty parlor looking for a job. I commented on what a great cook she was, but Ida already had it figured out. She explained that she had enough cash to open her own place, and she was going to hire Mickey as a receptionist. If Mickey wanted to do more, she could train to be a beauty operator.

She concluded by saying, "I believe she'd be good at it. She's got a lot of confidence, like her brother. When I lived in their place on South Street, I was welcome any time in her kitchen, and I know how sympathetic she is. Customers will like her."

Soon after this we had to leave. There was a two a.m. curfew on nightclubs, and I was home by three o'clock.

§

Friday was early closing. When the business travelers went home for the weekend, there weren't enough customers to keep the place open.

Ida came in just when I was about to close. She didn't offer to have a conversation with me. Something told me to leave her alone, to wait until she was ready to talk. She had a slick magazine and sat at the end of the counter reading it.

Henry Aldrich came in, a guy who had been giving me trouble for a couple of weeks. He was about forty years old, and I called him Henry Aldrich, because his voice was nasal and cracked; he was tall, thin, slightly stooped, with a large Adam's apple. Exactly my imaginary picture of the radio character *Henry Aldrich*.

He had gotten angry with me over something I couldn't even remember. Since then, he was angry every time he came in.

Henry walked up to the counter. He didn't sit down but stood glaring at me and said, "I'll have my usual."

Out of the corner of my eye, I saw Ida look up from her magazine. It was probably the angry tone of his voice that got her attention. I didn't take my eye from Henry.

I tried to remember what Henry had ordered in the past but didn't have the slightest idea. I knew this was going to be another episode.

I said, "I'm not sure what that is, Sir."

Henry's face puckered up and he said, "I come in here all the time. Are you too stupid to remember that?"

Ida popped to her feet like she just sat on a tack.

"Get out," she said to him.

Henry turned toward her with raised eyebrows and his face unpuckered. He didn't get a chance to speak.

Ida continued, "You heard me. GET OUT—NOW! Or I'm calling the police and saying you touched me and made obscene remarks."

Henry smiled at Ida. Not a real smile. A smile a rat might make leaving a sinking ship, if a rat could smile and wanted to.

He spun around and was out the door at a pace the equal of the four-minute mile, if he kept going that long.

I leaped over the counter and grabbed Ida in a big hug. "My hero," I yelled. "You scared the hell out of the poor bastard."

Ida sat down as quickly as she had jumped up. "I don't know what came over me. I just couldn't bear it. He reminded me of my father."

I took her hand, "Ida, let me thank you. I didn't have any idea how to deal with this jerk, and you put him away. Knocked him out cold. He's not coming back. Terrific"

Ida came back to her feet. Without thinking about what I was doing, I planted a big kiss right on her lips. When I did, she seemed to come out of her trance and said, "Thank you. I'll have some more, please."

She kissed me back.

We were standing, still in this embrace, when four high-school girls walked in. They were cheerleaders who came in often after their practice. The smallest of the bunch, a dark-haired girl of about five feet in height, said in a normal tone of voice, "Let's have an 'H', an 'O', an 'L', an 'L', and a 'Y' 'Holly', 'Holly', 'Holly'."

The others picked it up, speaking in unison.

I bowed and said, "Thank you, girls. Let me introduce my friend and protector, Ida Patini."

The girls rushed to shake hands with Ida and with me. For the next few minutes, there was some back-pounding and congratulations from each of them. Then, as quickly as the whole thing started, it was over, and they were gone.

Ida said, "I'm sorry for the way I was acting earlier."

"I thought you wanted some space. No apologies needed."

Ida said, "I have to go out of town, to Sanford, this weekend. I'd like it if we could go out again next week."

We made a plan to spend the day together on December 13th.

§

The next day, Sunday, everything changed. I was sitting in an eatery, one of those back-road places that smelled of flypaper year around, rolls of it hanging from the ceiling and wasted on these blue-collar flies that preferred meat and potatoes. They trooped around on the countertop looking for a meal, stalked by a man in a filthy apron, the owner, cook, waiter, and cashier. He tried to sneak up, swatting at them without much success.

His other defect of character was his taste in nonsense music. We were listened to a hillbilly beaut, a woman singing about how in exchange for a wedding ring she'd show a guy her tattoo. She made it sound like once he got to the tattoo he'd be next door to paradise.

Then came an announcer saying, "We interrupt this program for a special announcement. The Japanese have attacked Pearl Harbor. This morning at 7:58 Honolulu time, aircraft thought to have come from a Japanese carrier, arrived over Honolulu and began to strafe and bomb the harbor, Schofield Barracks and the city of Honolulu itself. Early reports are that the damage is extensive and that several, battleships have been sunk. The White House has announced that President Roosevelt will speak to the nation shortly. We return you to your program. Further announcements will be made as news becomes available."

The President spoke to Congress the next day and asked for a Declaration of War. He said, "Yesterday, December 7, 1941—a date which will live in infamy—the United States of America was suddenly and deliberately attacked by naval and air forces of the Empire of Japan."

I went downtown right away to enlist. I wanted to beat the rush.

Once I had gotten through the processing, they told me to report to the bus station at 6:00 a.m. on Wednesday, December 10th.

I went to see Torry Wode to quit the job.

Afterwards, I stopped by the beauty parlor and got Ida's phone number in Sanford.

When Ida came on the line, I told her I had joined up and would be leaving on Wednesday morning. I asked if I could write to her.

She said, "Are you kidding me? What d'ya think's going on here? You're not leaving without saying goodbye to me. I'll be back tomorrow afternoon, and I'll meet you at the soda fountain at 5:30."

§

I went out to Fontaine Street to say goodbye to LaBelle and started by giving her a big hug.

"Here you are leaving again, and you never properly told me about Asheville, what all happened up there."

"I was still on that WPA road crew. But in the end, I just got laid off. I should have brought you up there to see the mountains while I still had a job."

I didn't want her to get too far behind, so I told her about the fire, my trip coming back through Greensboro, and ended up by describing my soda jerking job and Ida Patini.

"This woman is from New York City?"

"Yes, near there, Tatie. It makes a kind of problem. She's way too advanced for me."

"I don't understand."

"Neither do I, and that's the problem."

She said, "Are you thinking of getting married?"

"Not right now. I'll be leaving in the morning."

"Where they gonna send you?"

"I'll know when I get there."

Labelle had work to do, and part of that time I sat on the back stairs while she was washing sheets.

We heard someone call 'Granbelle' a couple of times. Lana came around the corner of the house. A moment later, her friend Marla came around behind her.

The two friends were quite different one from another. Marla's eyes were darting to and fro, lively as a chipmunk's. Her eyes lit on me a couple of times, with interest, and then moved on again. When Marla looked at LaBelle, there was an expression on her face that I couldn't read.

But it was easy to see that Lana was quiet and anxious. Her head was tilted forward with her eyes down toward the ground for a moment and then looking up at LaBelle, like a person looking at a doctor who may be bringing bad news.

Meanwhile, LaBelle was staring at her granddaughter.

"Since you don't sleep here anymore, tell me where you do sleep now."

"At her house," she nodded her head in Marla's direction. "With her parents."

"Don't come here thinking to make a fool of me. Where you been staying?"

Lana didn't answer. For a moment, everyone was silent

Marla said, "Lana told you where we were. If you look like a fool, is that her fault?"

LaBelle gave Marla a big-eye look. "Don't get where you don't belong and ain't wanted."

Lana still had her eyes cast down. Then she looked up and said, "We been staying out at Old Tyler's cabin on Slippery Rock Creek. I didn't tell you 'cause I didn't want a big fuss, like we're having anyhow."

"Lana," LaBelle said, "this is a fuss that can't go on. I won't stand for it. You choose—a life here or out there. You don't have to do that now, but right soon you'll have to. Now, come say goodbye to Holly. He's off to war and needs us to pray for him."

"All right," said Lana.

LaBelle nodded her head forward, closed her eyes and prayed.

I couldn't help but see the restlessness of both girls. They fidgeted and looked all around except at each other. At some point, they each gave me an ugly stare, as if to say they wouldn't quarrel with LaBelle about it, but neither did they care whether I went off to war or not.

By the time LaBelle was done, the two girls had gone.

§

Ida and I settled into a booth and ordered vanilla malteds.

She told me her customers loved the President's speech to Congress. Some of them were afraid of an invasion fleet arriving off the coast of Southern California. Most thought the war would last a long time, but we would win in the end. Only one or two thought it would be over soon. She asked me what I thought.

I said, "Ida, from what I've heard, privates don't have opinions, just big appetites and sore feet. But, having said that, I do think it will be a long war, maybe ten years. What will you be doing while I'm gone all that time?"

"Doing? I'll be working on my beauty treatment and trying to set up my business. But, I don't want to talk about that right now. Do you really expect to be gone all that time?"

I wasn't sure how to answer her question. For me, it seemed that preparing for the worst was a good idea, but I didn't want to ruin her day with that. "All I can say about it, Ida, is that we were told we were in for the duration of the war—however long that might be."

It was not the right time or place for us to work anything out between us. As soon as we finished the malteds, I left to get ready to go. Feeling that for once in my life I had left Ida with something to think about, I went off to serve my country and to reflect on the wonders of Ida Patini.

§

When I entered the bus station the next morning, I saw four crowded benches. It was clear right away that most of these were my new mates, three-quarters of them were very young men, less than twenty-five years old.

Standing nearby were several important-looking, older gents carrying clipboards. I approached one of them and said, "Holly Rollins reporting, Sir."

He looked at me over his granny-glasses and said, "Don't call me Sir, rookie. Take a load off and wait for your call."

He looked at his clipboard, "Rollins, Holly. Board the bus heading for Birmingham, Alabama. They'll call it out soon."

He took a pencil from his pocket and put a mark on the sheet of paper attached to his clipboard.

I wandered between the benches to find a place to sit out the wait and heard someone call out to me, "Holly Rollins, you lucky son-of-a-bee."

The moment I heard the voice, I knew it was someone I'd known since we went through Wiley Grammar School together.

"Lucky to get a free bus ride, you mean, Chow?" I turned to see Powell Reddy coming my way. Chow sounds Italian. But I was just calling him by his nickname, Chowderhead, that he earned by his blunder-first-ask-questions-later approach to life.

"Damn if it ain't a free war. Helluva concept. I brought money to buy my own ticket, so this leaves me with spare dough. You want me to buy you coffee and donuts?"

"Good idea," I replied.

We went into the bus station café and took a seat at the counter. We ordered coffee and enough donuts to last a while.

Chow said, "Did you hear the scuttlebutt? You know we're heading straight for the Pacific war, don't you?"

"No, I just got here."

"I heard we're gonna go right into combat. Helping defend the Philippines."

"Who told you that? The Jap fleet's out there. How are we gonna get to the Philippines?"

"I know we're wasting time," he said. "This damn war'll be over before we can get into it at the rate we're going."

"Powell, what the hell are you talking about? We been in this war a few hours. The Blokes have been at it for two years already and got nowhere. The Chinese been trying to fight off the Japs for six or seven years and been getting all hell kicked out of 'em."

"That's right, Holly. You think I don't know that? But we're here now, and we're gonna settle this thing damn quick. Like 1918."

A loudspeaker announced our bus, and we were on our way.

During a twelve-hour stopover at Camp Shelby, Louisiana, Private Reddy and I, now Private Holly Rollins, were assigned to the First Battalion of Combat Engineers at Fort Ord, California.

When we finally got to Fort Ord on Christmas day, we were beyond worn out. For fifteen days, we had lived mainly on Trailway buses. I got so groggy I stopped getting off the bus to stretch. Only when I had to use the toilet. And even then, I was willing to wait all day.

Chow was worse. At each stop, he'd open an eye for a moment, then go back to sleep. How could he go so long without getting off? Must have a bladder as big as a melon.

At last we were there, and I hoped to be able to sleep. Instead, we got processed again, the third time. They started right in giving us shots again. One shot for each known human ailment. We ran the gauntlet between two rows of doctors who jabbed us until we had blood running down both arms.

We were taken to a large structure that looked to me like an airplane hangar and lined up at a Quartermaster's window. We were issued piles of clothing, boots, packs and other gear, and a rifle covered in cosmolene as hard as wax.

Finally, we all had our gear piled on the floor of the hangar and were standing around waiting for something to happen. Anything. That's when I heard a voice, loud, clear, and harsh. I turned, as did everyone in the hangar. Three men were standing by the open end of the hangar, in uniform, with Sergeant's stripes on their sleeves.

The one in the center stood a bit ahead of the other two. He was a black man who looked about the age of the mountains we had come through on the bus, old enough to have served with the Buffalo Soldiers who chased Geronimo through those mountains.

He was standing straight and still, wearing a cavalry campaign hat and three up and three down stripes. His service stripes, each representing three years of service, ran up his arm from the wrist. There was a trim moustache over his lip and a grim expression on his face.

He barked orders to us, having us separate into groups and count off by numbers. We were separated into five sections of sixty men, taken to barracks and assigned bunks. I ended up with a top bunk, next to Powell, also in a top bunk.

If there was a bugle call that next morning, I never heard it. The first sensation I had was of flying. My bunk was falling over and it crashed into Chow's bunk. The top of my bunk hit that one about midway and I came down squarely on top of someone I didn't know. He woke up and lashed at me with his fist, hitting me on the top of the head.

I scrambled off him onto the floor and then onto my feet. When I stood up, I saw Chow looking me over.

"What happened?" I asked him.

"You got tipped over," he replied. "By the Sergeant with the zebra stripes. He went into the latrine.

I looked down into the latrine and saw the Sergeant laying out his shaving gear.

I started to get dressed in a hurry. Everyone else did the same. All of us were dressed and standing by our bunks when the Sergeant came back through the barracks. Looking straight ahead and not at us, he walked through to the other end of the barracks to a doorway where he turned and spoke, in the same harsh voice we had all heard before.

"Every morning I'm going to come in here when it's time for reveille and turn the light on. Five minutes later I'm going to pass through here on my way to shave. Anyone still sleeping when I come through, I'm going to tip over. So, either learn to wake up or learn to fly."

With that, he left the room.

Chow turned his head to look at me and said, "I don't know his name. To me, from now on he's Sergeant Tipper."

The first week of training was not as difficult as I expected it to be. Sergeant Tipper was our Nanny Sergeant who marched us off wherever we had to go for training, left us, and came back to move us on to wherever we had to go next. And, of course, he continued to command our barracks and threaten us with turning over our bunks. He turned somebody over almost every day, and there was nothing to it. He just put his hand on the side of the top bunk and shoved. The weight of the bunk and men did the rest.

The days faded into one another. We were kept busy with training, exercise, marching, and firing range, up to eighteen hours in a day. From the end of training until reveille was time we had to ourselves, but we often had morning inspections that we had to spend half the night preparing for.

On one of these days, we marched five or six miles away from the camp to have grenade practice. We came to a cleared field in a pine forest, where there was a section of wooden bleacher seats. In front of them were two trenches, end to end, each about twenty feet long and four feet deep.

We filed into the seats. Sergeant Tipper was told to stay to help with the training because they were short-handed one instructor. He stood in front of the bleachers with three other sergeants.

They explained that a grenade is timed to blow up eight seconds after you pull the pin and release the safety handle. Under combat conditions this is way too much time, giving an enemy a chance to throw it back.

The instructors were out to teach us to pull the pin, release the handle, hold the grenade for four seconds, and then throw it. When the enemy picks it up, it's going to blow up before he has time to get rid of it.

They demonstrated how to hold the grenade and pull the pin. They warned us that when you release the handle, you have to clamp down on the grenade because the spring has quite a kick, enough to pull the damn thing right out of your fist to fall into the trench at your feet.

That very thing happened the day before in these same trenches, and the soldier who dropped it was killed when it blew up.

Everything went fine until Powell and I got in the right trench with Sergeant Tipper. We watched a soldier in the left trench take his turn. When the handle flew off, the grenade seemed to leap out of his hand and landed in his trench about ten feet away from him. The other three men in that trench dove out as this soldier walked over, picked up the grenade and threw it. In his haste, he let it slip out of his hand sideways, and it landed in our trench at the feet of Sergeant Tipper.

The good Sergeant was certainly the most experienced man on the field and might have come up with something. But Powell and I didn't give him that chance. On sheer instinct, we grabbed him by his arms and threw him out of the trench and dove out ourselves. Unfortunately, Sergeant Tipper had one boot still sticking over the lip of the trench when the grenade went off, and he got shrapnel in his ankle.

One of the other sergeants marched our company back to camp to do calisthenics. Later, we heard scuttlebutt that Sergeant Sledge, Tipper's real name, insisted on walking to the base hospital, where three pieces of shrapnel were removed. The doctors wouldn't let him walk out and insisted he stay off his feet for a few days.

The following Wednesday evening, Chow and I went down to the Post Exchange to get some extra supplies for cleaning the barracks. We approached through a parking lot out back of the PX. As we were sliding through a narrow space between a 1940 Cadillac and another car, we saw Sergeant Tipper sitting in the passenger's seat of the Caddy.

Both Chow and I turned around to look back, standing in front of the car. Something wasn't right. He didn't look like himself. Passing the passenger's window, I had seen him from only a couple of feet away. I could have sworn he had tears rolling down his cheeks and a look of misery on his face.

We looked at each other and went around to the other side of the car. I tapped on the glass with a coin. Sergeant Tipper heard me and looked over at us. He reached across and rolled down the window.

"Get in the back seat. It's open."

We got in.

For a few minutes nothing was said. He was facing forward, and we were looking at the back of his head.

I said to him, "We've talked over what happened, Sarge, and we're sorry as hell to have caused you to get hurt."

"Shut up," he said. "You're right. You owe me. I got something to say and I want you to listen. Shut up and listen."

We both said, "Yes, Sir."

"Don't call me 'Sir,' and I said to just listen."

We didn't say anything.

Another few minutes passed. Sergeant Tipper had a bottle on the seat and took a long pull. Then he began to talk.

"I was raised on a ranch in East Texas, near to Shreveport, loved horses and joined the Buffalo Soldiers at Fort Huachuga when I was just thirteen years old. Big enough was old enough back then, and I was already six feet tall."

Chow and I looked at each other. We'd guessed it. He was a Buffalo Soldier, by damn.

"We rode for days at a time chasing Apaches. Rustlers who ran off our horses and mules. Bandits from Mexico doing mischief in Arizona. We'd chase 'em back, all the way past Chihuahua City in Ol' Mex.

"I served sixteen years with that outfit and had it real good. We had a fracas now and then, enough to be interesting. And we had good mounts, excellent mounts. Arizona was hard on men, but deadly on horseflesh. Even the best horse could just drop dead going up the side of a mountain in that heat.

"That's where I did my best duty. With horses. I knew horses. Better than anybody else.

"Then, the Rough Riders asked me to make sure their mounts was good taken care of, and I went for it. Something new and different after sixteen years.

"That's when I come up on white trouble. I didn't grow up to it because I was on the ranch and never even went one day to school. We had white officers with the Buffalo Soldiers, but they fit in with us. No other way that could work.

"Anyway, I went to that Cuba War, to that Philippine War that went on and on until about nineteen and ten, I'd guess.

"I did my share. A good soldier. Nobody can say different. Was with calvary in the Great War, but they took our horses. We was really only mounted infantry by then anyhow.

"Now, here's this war and I'm fit as ever. I could whip you two babies, both at once. But they say I'm done."

Chow and I looked at each other and he asked Sergeant Tipper, "What do you mean, Sergeant? Did you retire?"

"Tomorrow is the end of my sixtieth year. They say I can't go on, even with the war. Not to be, they say. Not to be. That's why I can't thank you for saving my life. Yes, you did save my life. But you also put an end to it. You caused them to pull out my records and look me over. Wasn't nobody walking around saying how I was seventy-three years old. Not until all this happened."

Chow mouthed the words, "Say something" to me. I didn't know what to say, but I tried anyway.

"Sergeant, it sounds to me like you've done more than anyone else ever did. I can't believe there are many men before you who've done sixty years."

Sergeant Tipper grunted and took another pull on his bottle.

I tried again to make some kind of connection with him. "What kind of white trouble were you talking about, Sergeant?"

"What kinds, Private? I'd say, disrespect. That's big. Limits on service. Things you can't do. Will never do. Places you can't go. Will never go. But, disrespect. That's the most, the biggest. To me, anyway."

Chow said, "Sergeant, we both grew up with that segregation thing. This is the first time either one of us ever had a talk like this with a man of your persuasion, that is, a colored man of your type. So, we know all about segregation."

Sergeant Tipper said, "Son-of-a-bitch," in a voice even harsher than usual. He tried to throw open his door, but it banged into the car next to us. He closed it and started to slip across the seat.

He said, "You know so much about it. Good. Let me show you what I know about pulling heads off babies. Get out of the car, both of you."

Sergeant Tipper opened the driver-side door and got out. He was completely steady on his feet.

We both got out, but I didn't know what to do if he wanted to fight us. He was our Topkick. We'd be court martialed if we hit him.

Sergeant Tipper stood directly in front of us, looking us over from head to toe. After a few moments of this, he said, "January the first, eighteen-eighty-two. Sixty years."

We stood there, the three of us, continuing to stare at one another. I had no idea what the Sergeant might do.

"Get moving, Privates," he said. "Get back to your barracks."

Without waiting to see what we did, he eased himself back into the Caddy.

Chow and I went into the PX and did our shopping. Then we did go back to the barracks and spent half the night getting ready for an inspection.

When I finally got into my bunk, hoping for a couple of hours sleep before reveille, I thought about what Sergeant Tipper said about segregation. But I didn't know why he got angry over what we said. Somehow, it made me realize that maybe we didn't know beans about segregation. To us, it was a barrier we couldn't see over, around, or through. That's about all we knew about it.

The next morning, Sergeant Tipper was gone. We never saw him again.

Chapter Four

React to enemy contact by seeking cover and concealment.

----Combat Leader's Field Guide

Saturday April 1, 1943

While I was unconscious, the news of the stabbing appeared in newspapers around the country. General Fishbinder heard about it and ordered an ambulance be sent down to Raleigh to get me. That was another lesson in the power of the Medal. The Pentagon ordered the General to pass me on along to a hospital in Arlington, and he refused to do it, claiming I was too ill to be moved. But I think the General is a warrior who supports warriors.

The basic problem was that the knife wound had caused one lung to collapse and hemorrhage with a build-up of fluid in both. My health was not good due to poor nutrition and other debilitating effects of the tropical jungle and the diseases I contracted there. An initial surgery was done to patch up the wounds.

I was near death for weeks. Another surgery was done to relieve pressure on my heart and lungs. During all this time I was unconscious. One night a nurse came in to check on me and found I wasn't breathing. She sounded the alarm bells. Doctors and nurses rushed in and somehow managed to get my ticker ticking. No one knew, then or later, how long I was dead. A dreary view was that I would wake up with a brain like a cretin, one of the roads less traveled to purification. I was in a coma for a month following this incident.

§

Painful music of jungle parasites playing havoc with my insides woke me up. I tried to open my eyes. In spite of all effort, my eyelids remained shut tight as though they had rusted-up hinges. Meanwhile, my brain was starting and stopping, jumping here and there, rushing to nowhere. One thought was the pivot point of all this stirring around: 'Am I dead?'

Maybe a sniper nailed me on a bulldozer having my morning coffee. If I'm dead or was dead, it's odd I can't remember how it happened. Often I envied the dead after attacks continued throughout the night. That is, until the burial detail got to work. The holes dug in the swamp ground filled with stinking black water as they were dug, and each man wrapped in his blanket sank into that water.

These images froze my mind.

When I was four years old, I stood in the snow next to a box resting on two sawhorses above a hole filled with icy, black water. I remember I was trying to understand why my mother was in the box and to figure out how she would get out of it.

My uncles had two lengths of rope they were passing under it. Four of them got right up to the box and lifted it by the rope. Two other men removed the sawhorses from underneath.

My anxiety moved into my throat and chest, and I couldn't breathe as my uncles lowered my mother inside the box into the black water. What was going to happen to her? How could she get out of the box?

Then, the wooden box was gone, and my heart with it. The pain stayed with me. Now, here am I, waiting to be wrapped in a blanket and sunk into black water. I am sick of the stench of swamp water and of living in soil peppered with bits and pieces of dead comrades during month after month of banzai attacks.

War and putrefaction are the same thing.

Suddenly my eyelids lifted, but I couldn't see a thing. The light, though only a dim night light, was too much. Coming back from the dead is not easy.

When my eyes began to adjust, I squinted around and became aware of a face hovering about a foot above my own. This face had a W. C. Fields' bulb for a nose and eyeballs magnified by thick eyeglass lenses until each entire frame was filled with iris. I could see corpuscles moving in spider webs of blood vessels.

I closed my own eyes again. I'd rather be dead. At least, you know where you stand.

"Sergeant Rollins," called the face.

I didn't answer. I wasn't sure I could talk. Besides, if I'm dead, the voice must be looking for some other Rollins.

"Sergeant Rollins," the face called again.

"Am I dead?" My voice sounded a bit firmer to my ears, though still a whisper.

"Sergeant Rollins, open your eyes, please. We need to talk."

"Why?" I said with my eyes still closed.

"You were dead, just like you thought. That's what we need to talk about. I'm here to make a study, to find out how you were affected by that experience."

"Putrified."

The next time I opened my eyes there was a man sitting in a chair next to the bed. At that distance, his eyeballs had no more activity than Madison Square Garden on fight night.

I murmured, "I've got a pain in my gizzard."

"Sergeant Rollins, try to keep your eyes open and pay attention, please. I need you to stay awake for a few minutes. You've been asleep a long time, and I've been waiting to talk with you. Do you remember coming to this hospital?"

"Sure," I replied. "I was brought here from Guadalcanal."

"No, that isn't the right answer. You were brought here in an ambulance from Raleigh."

"They brought me all that way in an ambulance?"

"It's only sixty miles," the man informed me.

"From San Diego?"

"No, Raleigh."

"They were going to bury me in Raleigh, is that it?"

"Sergeant Rollins, try to avoid working yourself up, and let me explain a few things."

"I'll admit I'm confused."

"My name is Dr. Scott Windsor. I'm a psychiatrist making a study of special cases of amnesia, especially amnesia in men with recent combat experience. You may be a text book example, and we're excited about talking to you, to make that determination."

"Maybe my amnesia comes from being dead."

"Your case may not even be amnesia. Perhaps, being in a deep sleep has resulted in some confusion. My assignment is to help you recover, including but not limited to your memory. I'm not asking for you to do much, only for your cooperation. For example, tell me something you remember about Guadalcanal."

Was it my imagination, or was I being pushed into something way too fast. "Why are you asking me questions?"

"Sergeant, I want to see your state of mind. Find out if you know what's going on and can answer questions. Remember something for me, please."

"I remember lying in the mud after a sniper had killed someone. I remember being too scared to move but at the same time feeling stupid."

"Why stupid?"

"After firing, a sniper goes doggo. He's lying quiet hoping nobody spotted him. He's not going to shoot again right then. It would be suicide because in that moment everybody's looking for him. You might as well just forget about it and keep working, but instinct won't let you. Your body just throws itself down, and you can't stop it."

"What else do you remember?"

"Eating insects."

"Describe that experience, please. What was it like, eating insects?"

"It was like eating C-rations, only chewier and full of a bitter kind of sap."

"Why do you like to eat insects?"

"I never said I liked to eat them."

"Fair enough. Why did you eat insects on Guadalcanal?"

"When I opened a can of spam, they swarmed all over it, inches deep. I gouged out chunks of meat with my knife and then put the can down. When I brought the knife to my mouth, I passed it through a half-closed fist, scraping off as many as I could and ate the rest along with the spam."

The Doc stared at me as I told him this story. He looked like he was wondering if I needed shock treatments. "Sergeant, I'm going to have a dictograph taping machine set up here, and I want you to go back to the beginning and tell me about Guadalcanal. Then, go on from there to what you remember when you came back to the States."

"Doc, let me try to explain something. If you want a challenge, help me get away from there and to feel safe without a gun in my pocket."

118

"Sergeant, if you do what I ask, then you will know where you are and why."

What I didn't know when I woke up to find the Wizard of Death hovering over me was that Doctor Scott Windsor was on a Washington committee studying a condition they were coming to call *Combat Fatigue,* and I was his guinea pig.

He sent a letter to Red Carter asking him to fill out a questionnaire and also to mention any unusual behavior he had noticed since my return. The one that got the Doc's attention was Red's description of the epileptic attack.

He asked me to record a tape for him about the story I had been telling Red at the time of that seizure. I rasped a few tapes for him. I say 'rasped' because for some reason my voice was slow to recover. It felt like it had been drying out the whole time I was in a coma.

On the tape I told the same story I told Red, about the noise of combat and the snipers who preyed upon us at all times, when we were working on Henderson Field. I mentioned the infiltrators who came at night with knives. And I talked about Powell Reddy.

§

Ida and Red came down together several times to see me. The first time was while I was still unconscious. On their second visit, I was able to receive visitors.

"I told you to be careful!" That was the first comment Ida made on my recovery, blaming me for getting stabbed.

She added, "How can I look after you when you're locked up like in a prison?"

I didn't know what to make of her wanting to look after me.

Red asked, "Did anyone ever tell you what happened?"

I shook my head.

"The police arrested Leroy for attempted murder in stabbing you. Then, they charged him with the murder of Lana Blue."

I nodded to encourage Red to continue. "The police theory is that Leroy killed Lana during a quarrel among the three of them. They think Marla got away and went off with her parents. They're letting it out that they're going to be holding him in custody, figuring that Marla might come forward to testify against him. Even if she doesn't show up, they think they've got a circumstantial case against

119

him. The fact that he lied to the police and the Army, that he told us he had seen them after Lana was dead and Marla was gone. All of his efforts to mislead the police."

I cleared my throat and asked, "How do they know that Marla's still alive? Maybe he killed both of them, and her body hasn't been found yet?"

"The police thought of that," Red answered. "The witnesses out by Lana's place are firm in their claim to have seen Marla after the murder. So, unless he murdered them at different times, she is alive."

Ida said, "The trial is scheduled to start in a week."

She stood up and paced around the room, then added, "How are you going to be able to testify?"

As usual, she had asked the question I didn't have an answer for. I thought awhile about it.

I said, "Maybe I can get the General to have me taken down in an ambulance."

Red tossed in an idea, "Why not have the JAG take a deposition? That way, they could interview you here, and you wouldn't have to go to Raleigh at all."

Soon after, they were ready to go. Ida was already halfway out the door when she turned and said, "I almost forgot to tell you. Mickey sends her love."

Ida and Red left me alone with my worries about how I could testify.

In the end, the Prosecutor didn't do any of the things we thought of. I read about it in a newspaper. On the opening day of the trial, he told the press he was not going to bring me down to Raleigh. Gordon Carter had witnessed everything that happened the night of the stabbing. His testimony would be enough.

The trial lasted only two days. Afterwards, Red came over to tell me about it, but really didn't have much to tell. He was a witness and wasn't allowed to be in the courtroom. He said he had ordered a copy of the transcript for each of and was reserving judgment until then. But he did say that from what he had heard so far that no white man would have been found guilty of murder in the first degree on such evidence.

He thought the whole trial was an example of racism in North Carolina.

Marla never did appear, but the Prosecutor showed that he could manage without her.

Leroy was found guilty on both counts and sentenced to die in the electric chair, one month from the day of sentencing, the exact date to be set by the Prison Warden.

§

Doc told me he had reviewed all the transcripts and wanted to have a few sessions together to go over the things I had talked about, such as burials and the night Powell was killed.

First Session

We met in a small room furnished with two chairs and a table, plus a lot of recording equipment along the wall opposite the door. It was a room without windows.

Doc set up a reel-to-reel machine to record the session. He did that in all our sessions.

He started right in questioning me about the night Powell was killed. "What do you think about Powell's death now?"

I didn't handle it well, and I asked him, "What would you think, Doc, if you found your best friend in bed with your wife?"

That put an end to the interview.

Something did get through to me, and my brain started working around the clock, thinking about Powell.

Second Session

I couldn't help but believe that the Doc had a hard time being professional. He was still angry at my remark from our previous session. On a farm where I worked, we described someone like the Doc, someone who walks stiff-legged and bent over, as having a cob up his ass.

This time I got the jump on him. "What do you know about racism in the military, Doc?"

"It exists as much inside as it does on the outside. But, let's wait and see. The war may bring about a big change in all that."

Then, Doc got clever and asked me to describe, moment by moment, everything that happened the night Powell died.

I replied, "A large force, a regiment at least, maybe a thousand men poured through the area around Bloody Ridge, and for the first time since we had arrived on the island, they broke through our line. That ridge ran right down toward and onto Henderson Field. If they could get across the field and link up with the force attacking our left flank, we would be in desperate shape and could maybe be pushed into the ocean. My Combat Engineer Battalion was backing up that flank. We were re-deployed on Henderson Field to stop this linking up.

"Where I was positioned, we were only one company, but well armed in automatic weapons. We had at least six machine guns and ten Thompson guns were found somewhere. Powell and I were put into a sand-bagged, anti-aircraft position with a fifty caliber machine gun. They came in waves throughout the night. The large number of automatic weapons we had resulted in them being cut down as they attacked across the open, flat terrain."

"What happened to Powell?" asked the Doc.

"I'm coming to that right now. During the night some of the attackers got very close. That was when a hand grenade landed just behind me, near Powell. It exploded as he picked it up. His body shielded mine, and I had only a few pieces of shrapnel in my back. There you have it. That's Powell's story,"

I stood up and said, "And that's my story for the day. I don't want to talk anymore right now."

You could tell the Doc had more of his unending stream of questions, and I didn't care. I left there and went back to my room.

Third Session

Doc took up a new subject in this session, starting off with, "Could you tell me about the Japanese burials. It isn't clear to me. What about after the battle on the airfield?"

"Doc, you don't see things from the practical side. We were on an equatorial island. Don't you see what that means? With a few hours of daylight, that airfield would be unbearable with that many bodies rotting in the sun. We had to get rid of them as quickly as possible. Together with three other men, I raced off in the early morning light to get bulldozers. We started collecting bodies scattered over half the field and Bloody Ridge. We brought them to a collection point and piled them up. We got them into four piles, then each of us dug wide and deep trenches and shoved the bodies into these trenches and covered them up."

"In one of your recordings you talked about this, and I thought I heard you express some kind of remorse or regret over this incident. What was that about?"

"Doc, you're making me mad again."

"Sergeant, don't talk if you don't want to."

"You don't get how painful that was. Some of them weren't dead. That's what it was about."

"The Japanese soldiers, you mean obviously, weren't all of them dead. So, you took them prisoner, is that it?"

"Neither side took prisoners. We didn't have any room for them, and the Japanese don't believe in it. Also, I was mad about what happened to Powell, you understand? Maybe I ran over some of them."

"So, how do you feel about this, now?"

"Grow up, you son-of-a-bitch. Who do you think you're talking to?"

"Who am I talking to, Sergeant Rollins?"

I was really fed up this time. "Look at you," I said, "all puffed up with knowledge. Doc, you manipulate everything and aren't honest about anything."

"You brought it up, but you're not being honest now. Who am I talking to?"

"Okay. Let me tell you. Several square miles of palms were cut down crossing one another and filled with nests and holes, and camouflage. I was sent in to blow up trees, cut some pathways through all that. It was hopeless, too close in there to blow anything up, to treat the wounded or to disengage, too close even to use a rifle. After a week of slaughter, it ended up with thousands dead on each side. We won that battle all right because some of us walked out of there alive and none of them did. Who am I? A man whose nine lives are all used up."

I stopped talking, and the Doc wrote notes for a few minutes before commenting.

He said, "We all live in a trance of self-absorption, like sleepwalkers. Your horrible experiences have brought you out of that trance and into a new relationship with yourself and others."

"Doc, that's the first thing you ever said that I understood. You're right."

"What has happened to you is similar to a conversion experience. Those who have that experience are afterwards thrilled with all they see and hear, and feel like they're walking on air and seeing God wherever they look. They feel born again. But you don't seem to enjoy it that way."

"Maybe because in my eyes I am dead."

Once again, the Doc wrote his notes and then said, "Sergeant, you need to remember that you did really die in this hospital and did come back to life, right here. If anybody should know what there is to fear about death, it's you."

"So what. That's not what I'm talking about. The point is that hope kills your spirit, and living without hope restores it."

He was flustered. I could see it. He said, "Right now you are here with me. There's nothing to fear."

I jumped up, and as I left the room, I yelled, "It's all I've got. I'm not giving it up."

Fourth Session

The Doc got started in a new way. "Sergeant, I want to apologize to you. I know why you have been so often angry with me. I've been extremely insensitive at times in my questions and, I must admit, in my responses. I'm sorry. I have no experience in these matters. The fact that these events are appalling is the reason you are having problems with them. So, for me to react to the appalling aspects of them is unprofessional.

"I'm going to report to the committee that I can only help a patient when I've understood the life that patient was forced into. Where the events you describe were your everyday experience, you had almost to become a kind of psychopath to get through them."

He finished his apology by asking me, "Are you still willing to continue just a bit more?"

I felt somewhat wary of Doc right then, not understanding what he said about his apology. He was, after all, the master of manipulation. I asked him, "To do what?"

"Only one last question," said Doc Scott. "That night, the Medal night. Was there any particular emotion that you felt? Fear, perhaps, or anger?"

"I can only tell you that it's like remembering a nightmare, how I was that night, and how I felt. It's like I was taken over by a demon."

I knew there was more and waited for it because I didn't really know what it was. From an unexplored place inside of me it came, and I heard myself say, "I wanted to kill them. I enjoyed it."

The Doc had a grin on his face as though, for once, I had said something that fit one of his theories.

And that was the end of our sessions together.

During the next few days, I tried to figure out what I had learned and got no answer, but I did remember something. One day at the end of a conversation, I asked the Doc about it. "How about the fit I had, talking with Red?"

"That's what complicates your case. I believe that in one of those sleeping trenches you stabbed someone, perhaps a good friend. You've told me bits and pieces of this experience and had dreams about it. I have some ideas of a treatment we could do. It might not bring back the memories, but it might help even without that."

After this conversation, we had two stabbing sessions. We sat in quiet and darkness in his office until one of his assistants would throw the door open and yell. Doc and I, each of us with a rubber knife, would then begin stabbing the air and each other with these harmless blades. Sometimes we did this in silence. Sometimes we yelled as we jumped around in the semi-dark, while I sobbed and struggled for breath, half-blinded by tears.

I guess my conclusion about all this work with Doc Scott was that I didn't need to learn something about myself. It was about undoing something inside me that was knotted up.

§

I was dozing after lunch. The steam radiators were too hot to touch, and my room was too warm. It was permitted to crack open a window, but only at night.

There was a tap-tap at my door and Nurse Bobbi Reed opened it a few inches to whisper through the opening, "A visitor, okay?"

"No doctors, though. This is my day off."

A few minutes later, Chester came in and, to my surprise, I was happy to see him. Then, he sat down at the foot of the bed and would have sat on my feet if I hadn't jerked them out of his way. I couldn't help but compare that to the way he shoved my elbow off the armrest at the movies.

"Holly, I'm glad to see you. I've been reading about you in the newspapers for months now. Then I saw that report about you being stabbed at Mose Blue's store on South Street. How are you doing now?"

"Recovering, thank you, Chester. You say that name, Mose Blue, as though you knew the man. Is that so?"

"Do you mind if I smoke, Holly?"

When I nodded my agreement, he lit up a cigarette. "Yes, I've known Mose for years. He and his whole family, I should say. I used to stop by there about six or eight years ago. I stayed with Mickey and Buck at their boardinghouse a few blocks away on South Street and delivered liquor to Mose while I was staying with them."

"You say you knew the whole family? Who's that you're talking about?"

Chester took another drag off his cigarette before answering.

"You think you got an ashtray here, Holly?"

I took one from the table by my bed and handed it to him. "And the family?"

"Let's see. Maybe I shouldn't have said I knew them all, not being sure how many there are. But, I knew Lana, who was working there at the time. Then Jerome, a student someplace, but who came to unload and stack boxes, things like that. Once or twice when I was there, I met his parents. I believe they were called LaBelle and Old Tyler. I've always remembered that name because it sounds like bourbon."

"You knew Lana," I said. "Did you hear what happened to her?"

"No, I haven't," he said. "Nothing serious, I hope."

"She was murdered, and LaBelle asked me to look into it. That's how come I got stabbed. I happened onto the killer, Leroy Struthers, who worked there at the store."

"Leroy, the clerk?" said Chester. "I know him, used to see him when I came there."

"You say you were staying at the boardinghouse. Did you ever go down to that store with Buck or Mickey?" This whole connection was coming as a bit of a shock to me. Now I was wondering just how far it went.

"No, Buck was connected to my business only after they moved up to Asheville in 1939. I stayed with them because of our friendship and my feelings for Mickey."

"Maybe you can explain to me, once and for all, how involved you are in this effort to kill Buck." I set myself up to watch his every move, to see if he was telling the truth or just trying to sucker me into helping him find Buck.

"Holly, I'm a business man. Nowadays, more than ever—I mean since the FBI brought those racketeering charges against me. I don't travel anymore. I don't touch anything illegal. I'm like a company director, deciding on policy and establishing relationships with other businesses."

This guy should have been a politician. Rephrase that. I guess he *was* a politician. "Chester, you're not answering anything I ask you. Let's take it one thing at a time. Are you after Buck?"

"I was trying to answer, Holly. It's a business thing with me. He cost me a lot of money by helping the FBI. If I could, yes, I'd like to catch him and try to put him to work to get some of my money back. But I can't touch him. I'm surrounded by people who want to kill him."

"How about Mose? You're his supplier, right? You still see him?" I was, at last, getting something of a handle on Mister Slip and Slide.

"Sorry, Holly, I can't tell you about my business. I don't want to see you on the stand someday in yet another FBI or Revenue case."

Sonny and Anders came into the room. They brought in something dangerous and threatening. Sonny came to the left side of my bed, opposite to Chester, and Anders went to the foot. I felt like an exhibit on the hoof at the State Fair.

Anders, looking at Chester said, "Just as Sonny thought, Buck and Mickey both been here several times and another guy we might want to check out. Name of Carter."

In that moment I learned something about fear and my reaction to it. After five months of constant threat of being overrun and killed by the Japanese, lesser dangers lost some of their importance.

I said, "Two brave lads who murdered a passed-out drunk and now here to waste their time threatening me."

Chester, of course, spoke first, "You know that was an accident."

Sonny interrupted, "Chester wants to do his dance, and I don't blame him for it, but I don't feel that way. We want you to help us find Buck, and I want you to understand what's going on and where you stand. I set that fire. But first, I put an ice pick in that old man's ear and shoved it in until the handle was touching his eardrum. The old souse might have made a fuss if he woke up. When you see Buck, tell him how his old man died. Tell him he isn't neither going to hear from his sister in Lenoir. She was a cute little rabbit, and she's found a home in a rabbit hole out in the Smoky Mountains."

I told Sonny, "You are a perfect son-of-a-bitch, aren't you?"

"Listen to you," said Sonny. "We read about you in the papers. How many have you murdered, Hero? Buck condemned his blood, and they're walking dead."

I didn't feel the need to respond to Sonny and turned to Chester. "An eye for an eye, is that what this means?"

But Sonny continued, "This ain't eye for eye. All his blood must go."

There was a tap-tap at the door and Nurse Bobbi opened it a crack and poked her head through the opening to say, "Two more visitors waiting."

Chester beckoned to the other two men, and the three of them left without saying another word.

Moments later, Mickey and Buck came in and before they had a chance to speak, I said, "Did you see Chester, Sonny and Anders? They just left and must have walked by while you were in the visitor's room. You better watch out. They know you've been coming here."

Buck came instantly to a dead stop, motionless for a couple of seconds.

"I've got to find a back way before they get all the doors covered. Bye, Mickey, I'll be in touch. Thanks, Holly."

Buck left the room.

Mickey hung around for about a half an hour, so distracted by her worry about Buck that we couldn't carry on a conversation.

§

A week later I received a copy of the transcript of the trial, courtesy of Mayor Bats.

Lying there in bed, I read and re-read the transcript. There was enough to suggest that Leroy had some knowledge he was hiding, but not really enough to convict on a charge of first degree murder.

The day after I finished reading the transcript, Red showed up for a visit. I told him that I came to the same conclusion he did and we agreed that justice had not been done.

"LaBelle Blue sends her love," said Red. "Also, you should know that Old Tyler Blue died, and LaBelle is going to lose that property."

"What happened to Old Tyler?" I asked.

"He up and died is all. They had a big wake for him. She took down the sheets for once because she had more than one hundred people in her front yard. I've got a feeling they might have all been family. I believe the word is 'progeny.' When you live as long as he did, you can pile up a lot of them."

"Have you've seen her since? Do you know how she's doing?"

"I heard yesterday that she has to be out by the end of the month. It seems the grant of land on that property was to Tyler Blue rather than to LaBelle. Now the Fontaine family wants it back. Seems like they got an offer from a man who wants to put up an office building there."

For a long while, I couldn't sleep. I lay there and brooded about LaBelle and her future. After a while I switched moods and started thinking about my favorite mayor. By coincidence, Mayor Bats showed up the next day.

As usual, Mayor Bats came in talking.

"My boy, I was astonished when I heard what had happened to you. After what you survived in the Pacific, I couldn't believe it possible that you could get stabbed right here in town. I owe you an

129

apology for all your suffering. My police should have solved that case a long time ago, and that is the most galling thing about the attack made on you. They just don't work on murder cases where the victim is Negro, unless the killer is found standing over the victim shouting a confession."

Mayor Bats paused for a moment and I took that opportunity to break in, "Mayor, I need your help. LaBelle Blue has to move from the property on Fontaine Street. It was on a grant for life to her husband who just now died."

"Young man, let me give you a lesson in politics. I intend to be the next governor of this state. Newspapers all over wrote about you. Then there was wide coverage of the trial because of you. Your name is known in every household in the country. Anything I do to help you, I can announce to the press, and I get a windfall of press coverage for myself. Whatever you need, it's yours."

"I'm out of touch with LaBelle's situation because I can't see her while I'm in here. Could you find out what's going on?"

"Consider it done."

Mayor Bats appeared to be enjoying a confident self-approval. He stayed on for another thirty minutes, and we enjoyed each other's company.

That night as I waited for sleep to come I thought about Mayor Bats' comments about the lack of effort in the Blue girl murder case. A picture came into my memory of Leroy's face as he stood listening to my ranting at him the night he stabbed me. I went to sleep with that picture still floating around in my head.

In the fullness of time, as it turned out, my stab wound had helped me in an unexpected way. With the continuous rest, treatment and good nutrition in the hospital, my lungs got better, not only the wound but the fungus as well. The malaria went into remission, or whatever you call it. The symptoms stopped, and I seemed to be free of it, for the time being at least.

General Fishbinder's secretary called to tell me of an appointment at the Pentagon for a medical evaluation to determine if I was fit to return to active duty. General Fishbinder, with his usual generosity, sent a jeep and driver for the trip.

I checked in at the Pentagon desk indicated in my orders and was directed to a medical station where I was given a thorough physical and interviewed by a psychiatrist. They both gave me a thumbs-up.

When I went back to the Review Desk, hoping to get my orders, I was told they would be mailed to me within a week. They told me that my outfit was back on Guadalcanal in training for their next operation.

Good Lord, Guadalcanal. I could hardly believe it. That was the last place on earth I'd like to see. Too bad the Pentagon planners never asked me where I'd like to go.

The next day, back in Fort Bragg, my doctors signed my release. Since my duffel was still in Raleigh, I didn't have much to pack. I got it together and went over to say goodbye to General Fishbinder, a man who had been a true friend. The same driver I had on the trip to Washington took me to Raleigh.

I asked him to drop me off at the house on Whitaker Mill Road.

Chapter Five

*A threat is any source of danger to the Force with a
potential to negatively impact mission
accomplishment or degrade mission capability.*

----Combat Leader's Field Guide

Friday   May 15, 1943

Not wanting to add to Mickey's headaches by staying at her
house, I wrote her a note saying that I would stop by Saturday
morning at around seven, put my duffel into the A, and drove to the
Nash Hotel. The soda fountain where I once worked now had only
coffee and doughnuts, just what I wanted.

I knew my orders were coming soon, and I needed to wrap up
my efforts to help LaBelle. It didn't seem that I had done much for
her. The part I had played in finding Lana's murderer was like the
part a fly plays in feeding a spider. Nor had I done any better in
finding Lana's body. So far all that I had learned suggested the best
we could hope for was to find out what happened, but the body
would still be gone.

My third doughnut got a bit soggy in my coffee while I was
thinking over recent history. It was obvious that Sonny and Anders
were a threat to Mickey as well as to Buck. They said that Chester
wanted Mickey spared, but they didn't seem to agree with him on
that point.

Red, I was sure, shared a protective feeling toward Mickey
these days, what with Buck on the run and this uncertainty about
Sonny and Anders. I called him and left a message, to meet me at
Mickey's house before seven the next morning.

Who says odors don't travel far. I could smell Price's truck two
blocks before I got to Fontaine Street. From one block away, I could
hear loud, arguing voices. When I came to the street, I saw the man
himself standing by his truck with his back toward me, being
harangued by his neighbors.

I soon learned one of those big lessons. This one was that anger
is easily transferred from one cause to another. A wise man would

have remembered the neighborhood curtains and the sniper eyes behind them and simply crossed the street and gone on to talk with LaBelle. A fool would walk up to the group and try to have a word with Price.

I recognized most of the five neighbors. There were the Wankys, a mother and daughter living two doors down from Price. The Primes, from next door to him, were a brother and sister, both recently divorced and, as I found out later from LaBelle, trying to survive living together in middle age. The other man I didn't know then but learned later was the man living in my old house and owner of the fence.

As I walked past Price, I tapped his shoulder. Even as he turned, the others shifted to line up behind him. In the blink of an eye, they were united as a group, focused on me and very unhappy. I played the fool.

I said, "I wanted to thank you in person for passing on the message from LaBelle Blue. It has meant a lot to me."

Mother Wanky wasn't able to contain herself any longer, "What are you thinking, Rollins, contributing to the blight on this neighborhood?"

"You mean this truck?" I said. "Ask Mister Price, here, if I had anything to do with it."

Daughter Wanky grabbed the floor next by saying, "You know very well we're talking about that Negro across the street. You're helping her, and everyone here knows it."

LaBelle's neighbor added, "We don't want her here, and we sure as hell don't want you interfering with us."

A flare of anger went off in my chest like a mortar round. But, maybe I wasn't entirely a fool, because I knew instantly such a mistake could cost LaBelle. I said, in a quiet voice, "I'm on a medical furlough and not interfering with people right now."

I guess I wasn't entirely ready to let it go, because I added, "I even forgot my pistol in my other pants."

Price pulled a tactical move that saved the day. He stepped forward, beside me. This simple action destroyed the group. Next, he broke up the lynch party by saying to me, "Let's take a walk around the block."

How welcome that sounded. I really didn't want to battle with neighborhood watchdog grandmas. We didn't go around the block. By the time we got halfway to the next corner we were out of things to say and came back to find the neighborhood at peace again.

LaBelle had come out into her front yard with a large wicker basket posed on her hip, getting ready to hang sheets. She seemed even more pleased to see me than when I first came home. I hoped that Bats managed to give her some confidence about her future.

She put her basket down as she said, "Moon, it's good to see you on the mend. Good Grace, you were like a dead man."

We gave each other a big hug.

"Tatie, maybe grace is the right word. There I was in desperate condition, needing rest and recovery, and along comes Leroy and gives me that chance without even being asked."

"I see you got your sass back, not that you ever needed any help with that. I want you to know that your friend Red came to see me once a week to tell me how you were doing. Mostly, he came by after coming up to see you. The Mayor came, too. First, tell me, how are you doing now?"

"I'm doing well enough that they're sending me orders to return to active duty. I should be going back in one or two weeks, meaning it's time to finish what we started about Lana."

LaBelle had that challenging look in her eye. She said, "Tell me what's going on, then?"

"I was thinking during last night and today about where we stand. I went about it all wrong. Parker is the man we need most to help us, and I got him so riled up, all he can think of is shooting me with his Police Special."

In that tone of hers that leaves no doubt, LaBelle said, "This ain't about you, Moon. Nor even about me. It's about Lana. You got to get right about this. We can't count on police help. She's in a hole someplace, and we got to find her."

Leaving her basket and unfinished work, she headed toward the stairs. I followed her into her house and into the kitchen.

She went to the stove, lifted the plate and spit into the flame. She turned and fixed a gaze of iron on me. "She's put in some dark and lonely place. Maybe it's not even a grave. That's what you got to find."

LaBelle turned back to the stove, lifted the plate a second time, and spit her snuff into the flame. This time she didn't replace the plate right away and I could see the flame licking the edges of the hole.

"Maybe they cremated her, Tatie."

"No, they wouldn't do that. We got to bring her home and bury her right."

I'd had problems before with the heat in this kitchen. I felt as though I might have to suffer through all that again. But nothing happened. Maybe I really was well at last.

LaBelle was waiting for me to say something, to come up with an answer somehow. To buy time, I asked her, "Did you ever know of any connection between Lana and Leroy?"

She shook her head, very slowly. "I can't imagine that. I know Leroy. Before the war, I used to go to that store once a month. Never saw the two of them show any interest at all. You got to know that Lana's smart. She's never liked dumb ones like Leroy. I bet Mose lost a lot of money because Leroy can't even make correct change."

"Red and I both read the transcript of the trial. We think he didn't get a fair trial."

LaBelle said that she had attended every day, sitting in a tiny section of the balcony labeled 'for coloreds only' in the segregated courtroom. "I'm going to tell you about the fair trial he had. There were two charges, he stabbed you, and he murdered Lana. They proved he stabbed you, and that's all they tried to prove. This was pure white folks, all about you and nothing about Lana."

"I don't understand, Tatie. What do you mean pure white folks?"

After having freshened up her snuff, she spit into the stove and replaced the lid. She turned to look me in the eye and said, "Because Leroy is going to be executed for stabbing you. It ain't got nothing to do with Lana. They barely even proved he knew her, because like I told you all along. They don't care about a Negro girl, even a beauty like my Lana."

What she said hit me like the wave that causes a ship to founder, driven under water by the force and weight of it. It struck me instantly as true. Maybe I had known it all along without knowing that I knew it as I read the transcript. Since the landing on the beach of Guadalcanal, I had moved between the poles of anger and fear.

Now, two new emotional poles opened up, a feeling of kinship with Leroy and a sense of guilt for what was happening to him.

I didn't know how to respond to her. I asked a question instead, "What did the Mayor have to say?"

"The Mayor wants me to be his housekeeper."

"That's wonderful. Are you going to do it? You'll do a great job there."

"If you think so, I'll do it. I know you talked the Mayor into giving it to me."

"No, Tatie, the Mayor did this all himself. You made an impression that day we had lunch with him. I know this will work. Both of you are very straight in dealing with other people. He likes to make people think he's weird, and he is weird, but behind that, he's an honest guy."

When I left LaBelle shortly afterwards, the old familiar feeling that nothing had been resolved was gone. I didn't know what to say or what to do about what, but I did know that everything was now different.

§

The next morning I was happy when Red showed up at quarter to seven and quick to let him know that I was worried about Mickey.

"I've been here for only a few minutes, Red, but I tell you it's not right. After twenty years of cooking breakfast, she always gets up at four-thirty. But, the house is dark and no sign of anything."

While I was talking, Red was studying the house. "What should we do, Sergeant? Got any tactics to cover this situation?"

"Yes, Red, I do. You go around to the back, right up close to the back door. I'll wait two minutes for you to do that, and then I'm going in the front."

Red went off through a gate to the side yard on the opposite side to where the Model-A was sitting just outside the fence.

After two minutes, I started toward the front door. Then I heard a rustling from the side yard, like something coming fast. Over the fence came Red, head-first, with exactly the form he used to score against a goal-line defense. He finished a somersault, coming up onto his feet and in the same movement started into a trot to where I was watching him.

"Holly, Mickey's got a bobcat that almost had me for breakfast. As I was coming across the back of the house, I looked down the lawn and saw a sight I don't ever want to see again, that bobcat coming up from the back of the yard like a freight train, except not making a sound. When it was about ten feet away, it made its move, leaping towards my throat. Holly, you know how quick I am. I jumped to one side and, as luck would have it, I was standing directly in front of the cellar stairs. Down the bobcat went and crashed into the cellar door, giving me just enough of a head start to make it to the fence with that cat burning grass right behind me. Now comes an even weirder thing. As I was in the air, I heard that bobcat chuckling. To him, my tailbone going over that fence was funny."

The watchdog cat. I forgot all about him.

"Red, you just ran into the business end of Mickey's giant, wacko tabby. Name of Joe. She said not to mess with Joe."

"Believe me, Sergeant, I ain't gonna mess with that sumbitch."

"I've always wondered what he could do. I think you'd have been a tattered and torn buckaroo, if Joe hadda got hold of you. Let's both go in the front door, right?"

"I ain't gonna argue with that," Red nodded.

When we got to the front door, we found a rolled up bit of paper tied with string to the door handle. It said, "Ida telephoned last night to come in this morning to clear up. They had a big mess last night. See you at Bad Dad's after three o'clock."

Thus ended the Joe affair, which gave Red a chance to show he still had something in the tank.

§

Mickey and I played at our favorite table, the last one in the back. Like the other tables, it was streaked with cigarette burns and looked older than it was. We liked this table above the others because it had fewer dead spots in the cushions. Also, the other tables were so close together you had to wait while some sun-wrinkled redneck in worn overalls tried to decide what to do. With a game costing only a nickel, pool was the cheapest entertainment in town, especially if you're dead-slow playing it.

We were having a good match, playing even. Red was sitting on one of those high stools watching us play.

I became aware of that dreaded mood settling over Mickey as it sometimes did. She started to swish around the table, slamming balls into the pockets and ran the table in under a minute and won our bet.

It was a warm evening. Red, Mickey, and I went out front where Bad Dad had wicker chairs on the sidewalk. He put them out at five o'clock when the shops closed. The sidewalk emptied within a few minutes. After that, the neighborhood was calm and quiet.

Red asked Mickey if she had heard anything about Buck, or about Chester or the others, the Boozer twins.

She said, "The truth is that Chester and I were engaged until just a couple of years ago. I can't believe he would hurt me. You should forget about him. If there's any threat to me, it can come only from Sonny and Anders, and not from Chester."

Red answered her, "That's good to know, Mic. We'll focus on them from now on."

§

Monday morning I went to the police station and asked to see Lieutenant Cabot. "I need to talk to those detectives again, the ones who worked on the Blue girl case."

Lieutenant Cabot consulted a duty roster before responding to my request. "Sergeant Winter is here and can answer your questions. The only condition I have is that you tell me why you need to see him again, especially with the trial already over."

"I spent some time trying to find Marla Brown, without any success. Now, I'm beginning to wonder about it. Where is she? Why didn't she come forward? Is it possible that Leroy killed them both, but at different times? I wanted to discuss these issues with your detectives. I also want to report some criminals I know to be here in town, men responsible for a murder in Asheville a couple of years ago."

He asked me a few questions and ended up arranging for me to see Sergeant Winter.

When I got to the Sergeant, I went through the same spiel for a few minutes. He interrupted to ask, "What do you want from me?"

"I guess I want two pieces of information from you, and I want to give you some information. First, did you ever run across any hint where Marla Brown might be? Second, did you find out anything more about Lana Blue's body?"

"The Sergeant began to shuffle some folders around. "We never found out where Marla Brown was living at the time. We found only where she had lived up until some months before all this happened. And I have no new information on Lana Blue. What was it you wanted to report re a murder in Asheville?"

It took me about ten minutes to go over the history of what happened in 1941, the saga of Chester, Sonny and Anders. The story of Buck's father, who was stabbed by Sonny. Then, I went on to the threat to Mickey and the fact that Red and I were working to keep her safe and ended by informing him that I was called back to active duty and could not continue to guard her.

The whole visit was a waste of time. Sergeant Winter, though sympathetic to our situation, told me there was nothing they could do. They had no jurisdiction on the Asheville crime nor any request to pursue any suspects or fugitives. They couldn't assign anyone to guard Mickey until an assault had been actually made against her.

In the end, he wished me luck in the war, and I thanked the Sergeant for his patience and help.

I left feeling agitated and uncertain what to do next. It seemed a good time to stroll around town like I did when I first got back to Raleigh and try to come up with something.

Somehow I was drawn back to Capitol Square, just a few blocks away. Looking now at these memorials I wonder why people cherish these memories of suffering. Maybe they needed to just let it go.

I found myself standing in front of the *White Only* and *Colored Only* water fountains. When I saw these signs before, I didn't think about the threats and violence behind them. Is this what we are fighting for: people treated as untouchables or a young woman beaten to death without anything being done about it? I could feel a deep anger stirring around inside me, and disgust settled into my stomach like a feeling of nausea. There was a newspaper stand nearby, and I bought one and sat down on a bench to see if I could find anything about Leroy's appointment with the electric chair. Was he allowed visitors or would he be secluded even from other prisoners? I found no mention of Leroy in the paper. I thought about telephoning Leroy's lawyer. He would know if I could see Leroy.

§

Nathan Rose had a small office off Wilmington Street. His secretary said I could come at 3 o'clock, when he would be getting back from court. She showed me into his office at 4:15.

I told him what I wanted to do.

"In my opinion you would be wasting your time going to see Leroy. He blames you for everything that has happened to him."

"But I know some of this is my fault. That's why I want to talk with him."

When I came in, Nathan had been filling his pipe. Now, he took his time to fiddle with it just right and light it up. He sighed and said, "I've been dreaming of this moment all afternoon, Sergeant. I can't help but enjoy it. Now, I'd like to be clear on an important point here. If I had defended Leroy on the sole charge of murdering Lana Blue, he'd have gotten fifteen to twenty years, maximum, and out in ten. Providing, of course, that the State had a case. They didn't feel the need to present one in this trial."

I had the uncomfortable feeling that what LaBelle said was the truth. "Why didn't they present one?"

"This was a segregation trial, pure and simple. Leroy stabbed a white man, not only a white man but a war hero, not only a war hero but just after he was paraded down main street in front of God and everybody. Leroy never had a chance."

I said, "I'd like to see him, if it's possible."

Nathan puffed on his pipe, giving me a dead-cold stare.

"Sergeant, I'll make you a deal. I'll get you in to see Leroy, providing that he agrees. In exchange, I want you to be present for his execution on Friday. I'll put your name on the list and expect you to be there. Leroy is right in holding you responsible for this whole situation. So you need to come."

"You're going too far. I'm not taking that much responsibility. He did murder Lana, and he did stab me. But I'll agree to your terms, and I will come to the execution."

He said, "Please, wait a minute in the outer office, and I'll go ahead and call him now."

141

I sat down in the secretary's office, expecting to wait awhile. In no time, the lawyer came out and announced: "He surprised me. He wants to see you. You need to go right out to the State Prison because visiting hours are over in one hour. Do you know where it is?"

"Sure, I'm on my way."

I drove down Hillsboro Street to the State Prison.

Leroy Struthers came into the visitor's room and sat down opposite me. We were separated by a perforated-glass panel.

"What d'ya want?" asked Leroy.

"I wanted to tell you that I understand what you did."

"You understand."

"Yes, I do. And, I wanted to ask you if you know what happened to Marla?"

"Why should I tell you anything?" asked Leroy.

I was my most patient self. "That's why I came out to see you, to ask you this question."

"Maybe so. D'ya wonder why you're here, why I let you come here?" Leroy was looking more and more belligerent.

"No, I don't."

"So's I could tell ya myself to go to hell." Leroy started to get up a head of steam. "Ya're the one got me all this trouble to start with. Now, ya come in here to tell me ya understand. Well, understand this. I'm sorry you ain't dead, then I would know why I was here."

Leroy got up and started to leave the room.

I called after him, "How about Cotton Jimson? Did you kill him, too?"

Leroy turned around and looked at me.

"I remember when you was working the pin-boys like a big-boss. I didn't like you then, and I don't like you now. But you know what? That don't even matter anymore. This is the chair. You know that a man cook like a chicken. Meat come off the bone the same and the eye bust open like a roast berry."

Then, he turned to leave the room. The interview was over. As he went through the door, I heard a harsh and eerie laugh.

§

There were seven people ahead of me when I got to the gate of the State Prison. The execution was scheduled for six p.m., and I had been told to be there forty-five minutes early to undergo the security check-in. A door in the gate opened at five-fifteen, and we went in. There was a reception window on the left-hand side of the narrow room we filed into, with a waist-high rail that forced us to pass in single-file by the window. The process went smoothly. They checked our identification papers, confiscated all our pocket materials and purses, and searched us as the final step. We then passed down a very narrow hallway and entered the observation room.

This room had folding chairs and a closed curtain along one wall. It was only about twelve feet long and eight feet wide, with something of the feel of a room down in the bowels of a battleship. There were fourteen chairs, placed in two rows of seven. These chairs completely filled the room, and the observers were touching elbow to elbow and knee to knee. When they opened the curtain, my first impression was that the chair could have come out of a Frankenstein monster picture. It was a raw, functional, ugly, green chair with open straps hanging from the chair's arms and legs. On the opposite wall were several panels of gauges.

Then, the curtain was closed again and remained closed for about fifteen minutes. When it opened the second time, Leroy Struthers was strapped into the chair with a wired plate strapped to the top of his head and with wired straps attached above his ankles. I watched his face as one of the guards read out the charges and findings against him. I'd have to say that he looked as though he didn't know what was going on.

When the guard had finished reading, he approached Leroy and snapped a veil across Leroy's face. At that moment, I didn't know where to look and so, I didn't see the switch thrown the first time. What I saw was that Leroy's body suddenly seemed to rise up out of the chair and was held by the straps. But his back arched quite a bit, and his entire body looked full of the force of the electricity, straining every muscle to the maximum until his whole body was stretched out and yet completely rigid.

After what may have been only a few seconds, the current was shut off and Leroy's body settled back into the chair. Two men I

143

hadn't noticed before came forward from the far corner of the room, a guard and a doctor. They both stopped by Leroy, and the doctor examined the body and announced, "Leroy Struthers is not dead."

Unbelievably, the whole process was repeated a second and then, finally, a third time before the doctor proclaimed Leroy to be dead at last, as done as a holiday bird coming out of the oven. We could smell the cooked corpse in spite of the apparently solid wall separating us from the execution chamber.

§

I walked across town to visit LaBelle. It seemed something to do, to tell her what I had seen. But I wasn't sure what to say to LaBelle about Leroy's execution. Even after all the horrors of Guadalcanal, seeing an enemy soldier running around covered with burning oil from a flamethrower. Even after all that, my stomach was churning from watching what happened to my old colleague, the Tonk-addicted pin-setter.

When I turned onto Fontaine Street, the first thing I saw was LaBelle's neighbor sitting on the ground surrounded by pails and brushes, everything a happy homeowner needs to do a job of whitewashing. I stopped on the sidewalk near him and said in a pretend-polite tone of voice, "How do you like your fence, you son-of-a-bitch?"

"How come you to call me that?" He put down his stirrer and stood up. "What do you want?"

Noticing a hammer on the top shelf of his toolbox, I grabbed it and struck one of the boards three times, quickly and with a lot of force. On the third blow, the board gave way and split vertically where I struck it.

The neighbor began screaming to someone in the house to call the police. Almost at that same moment, LaBelle came around the fence. I saw her out of the corner of my eye as I set to work on the next board. The man was still screaming about the police. Now, LaBelle started screaming, "Stop it, Moon. Stop it."

I kept pounding on the fence, determined to break it down board by board.

LaBelle tried to cut me off by sliding along with her back to the fence. The neighbor grabbed her and starting trying to pull her away from the fence.

I ignored them both and just moved along to another board and began working on that one.

A police car slid to the curb when I was on my fifth board. Two men leaped out. One was a uniformed patrol officer and the other was Parker Reddy. Parker told the officer, "Grab the woman."

LaBelle was struggling still with her neighbor when the officer wrapped his arms around her. The very instant he pinned her arms, the neighbor launched a wild swing and clipped her right on the jaw. Down she went, not all the way to the ground because she was held up by the officer.

I had seen and heard the whole thing, even with Parker yelling in my ear. That did it for me. My cup runneth over. I turned toward Parker, with the hammer in the lock and load position, ready for action. He was an experienced police officer. He saw a change come over me, saw me turn and start for him. Wisely, he backed off. I began to stalk him. He continued backing away.

I began to talk to him. "You want to know what happened to your brother. He didn't die like I said. After he was wounded, he begged for his life all night long. He wept for his Mommy, saying over and over that he didn't want to die. He pleaded with me to come help him. But I didn't. I just let him die."

"You're a liar." Parker turned to see that LaBelle was sitting up. He said over his shoulder to her. "You looking for Lana? Want to know where she is now? She's in the garbage, in a mass grave in a pile of worthless, jigaboo drunks."

As he finished, I looked over towards LaBelle. Even in her half-conscious state, her face registered shock. I took off in Parker's direction. He backpedaled as fast as he could, but I was catching up with him in a hurry when the lights went out. Much later I found out that the uniformed officer laid me out with his billy.

A few minutes later I woke up with my head cradled on LaBelle's lap in the back of the police car. The uniformed officer was driving, and Parker was in the front passenger seat. Parker was saying, "Let's just leave them at the door as soon as Rollins wakes up. I don't want any paperwork over this, and you shut up about it."

145

§

LaBelle and I were left in front of the Emergency Room entrance. We walked through the doorway and found ourselves in a large room with benches, easy chairs, tables with magazines, and a desk labeled *Information*.

We approached the nurse sitting on the other side of this desk and I said, "I believe I may have a concussion. Could I get checked out, please?"

The nurse opened a drawer, pulled out a form and pencil, and said, "Please, give me your name and address, and tell me why you're here."

She looked down at her paper with her pencil poised to write. Then, she looked up and added, "This Negro woman can't come in here with you. She has to leave the hospital."

"I need her with me because I'm not steady on my feet. I was just knocked out cold."

The nurse got to her feet. "We can get you a wheelchair and take you back in that. But, this woman cannot be here. This is a white-only facility. That means she needs to leave right now."

"Close relatives," I said. "That counts for something, doesn't it?"

"Mister, you still didn't give me your name," said the nurse. "But what difference would it make since she is obviously not a relative? I'm going to call a security guard if she doesn't leave right now."

LaBelle tugged at my sleeve, and I took her hand.

"Moon, I'm going. We've had enough trouble for one night."

I looked at LaBelle and then, turned to the nurse.

"Moon, that's my name," I said to the nurse. "Moon Blue. Put that on your form. And put down that I live at seven twelve Fontaine Street with this woman, my grandmother, LaBelle Blue."

"Are you saying this Negro woman is your grandmother?"

"Yes, I'm Moon Blue, and she is LaBelle Blue, my grandmother."

"Just a moment, please." The nurse left her desk and went through the door to the Emergency Room, re-emerging from there only moments later with a hospital guard right behind her.

146

She stopped, turned half-way around, lifted her arm and pointed toward us with a gesture as dramatic as a scene from *Uncle Tom's Cabin.*

"Take these Negroes out of here," she told the guard.

Before he could get to us, I said to her, "Nurse, we're fighting a war for freedom all over the world. And now, right here. Praise the Lord and pass the ammunition!"

She responded by yelling at the guard, her face turning red, "Get them out of here this instant."

The guard took each of us by the elbow and led us to the door and out onto the sidewalk. "Get moving and don't come back," he said.

LaBelle and I walked back to her place. I was still dizzy with a large headache. When we turned into Fontaine Street, we saw a group of people standing on the sidewalk talking. In the center was the owner of the damaged fence. We stopped about six feet behind the group who were blocking the sidewalk. First one, then another, and the whole group turned to face us. It was the Wankys and the brother and sister Prime. Even Price was standing in the back of the group.

The owner pushed through his neighbors and rushed up to me. "I'm sending you a bill for this. It'll cost twenty dollars at least to repair the damage you done."

LaBelle and I stood directly in front of the man. I said, "I'll pay your damages. Send the bill to the lawyer, Nathan Rose. He's in the phonebook. Now, please, step aside." With that, I took LaBelle's arm, and we began to walk forward. The man had no choice but to step to one side. The group behind him followed his lead, and LaBelle and I walked the gauntlet of hostile stares.

When we entered her home, I was surprised and happy to see Mose there.

"Mose, we just had a great victory at the hospital," I said.

"Victory, what kind of victory?" Mose asked.

"I don't rightly know. What was it all about, Tatie?"

LaBelle said, "Our preacher did a sermon on Mohat Mogandi, that India man walking around in sheets like these here. Our heads got busted, and we got put out of the hospital by an armed guard. That would be just about right to count as a victory to the great

Mohat. If you keep on like this, Moon, when they lay you down, they'll say, "Here lies Brother Rollins, may he resist in peace!"

"I'm not sure what that means, Tatie, but I'm not putting up with you being treated like that."

"Don't fret no more about it, Moon."

"But Tatie, I was a selfish fool to grow up here without thinking about what you go through every day. And now, especially, that we're fighting a war for freedom."

"Moon, you're talking over your head now."

"Those *White-only* and *Colored-only* signs downtown make me sick."

"It's better you don't have a say about all that."

"I don't understand this, Tatie." I felt lost in the way she seemed to keep turning everything back toward me. "What are you telling me?"

"We been close since the beginning, and you can't bring all this in. Not if you want us to carry on as before."

"I still don't understand,"

"Go off and think on it. Moon, I was angry at the hospital. But, I've come home to peace now. Do you understand me?"

"No, I don't."

"Mohat says hatred is overcome by love. If you fight it, you only make it grow. To me, he sounds just like The Lord Jesus, walking in the truth."

"I don't know much about him, besides seeing him in the newsreels. I think you're talking about Mohat Gandi."

"I'm talking about hatred's fever and torment. I watched it all my life. I know its ways. And so does Mohat know its ways."

I felt deeply disappointed by what she was saying. She seemed to accept this evil. I could admire that she didn't seem to be defeated by it, but I couldn't be satisfied to have an attitude like hers.

LaBelle took my arm and turned me to look at her.

"You told me to think. About what?"

"I should have told you to go away and don't think about it."

"I don't see how you can decide to give up. There are battles we need to fight. We can't let the Japs and Nazis take over the world. We're in a war to end all wars."

"It's not my job to decide about war or the world. My job is to praise The Lord and wash sheets."

LaBelle spoke in that firm, stern way she had.

Then, she added, "I want peace in my house. Listen to Mohat, and don't bring that stuff into your heart. And if you do, don't bring it into my house."

"All right, Tatie."

I finally saw that I was wrong about one thing. Though her reasons were beyond my understanding, I could see that LaBelle Blue was not about to be humiliated, anymore than Mohat was. That part was good to hear and made me feel proud of her, proud to know her, proud that we loved each other.

I left right after this conversation. I was too worked up and restless to continue talking about what had just happened. I needed to take a walk and let it all settle down.

§

Ida telephoned to the Nash Hotel the next afternoon and said, "Can I meet you at the diner? We need to talk."

"I'll see you there in fifteen minutes."

I got to the diner a couple of minutes ahead of Ida and took a seat at the far end of the counter from the other patrons. She soon joined me, and we each ordered toast with honey and hot tea.

"Two men began hanging around in front of the Parlor a few days ago. I asked the girls if they knew anything about them. Mickey came to me and said they were looking for Buck. I think Buck conned some money out of a bootlegger or something like that.

"Then this morning, they threw a brick through the Parlor's front window with a note that said, 'Where's Buck?' That did it for Mickey. She took off out the back door."

"The question is, what do you want, Ida? I mean, what do you think you can do about this situation?"

"I'd like to do something, but I don't know what. I don't know where Buck went, for starters. Maybe you've got some idea."

"My idea is to walk you back to your Parlor, to see if the two men are still there, unless you happen to know they're already gone."

"All right, I'd be relieved to know they were gone."

Ida and I walked back to the Parlor. She pointed out where the men had been seen loitering before. Nobody was there. I walked around the neighborhood for about an hour looking for anything out of the ordinary, but didn't see anything of the kind.

I ended up going back to the Parlor and leaving an All Clear message for Ida.

I went to Mickey's place to keep watch there. When I got there, it was already getting dark. I parked the car and settled down to wait to see what happened next. To my satisfaction, a light suddenly went on in Mickey's place. At least, I wasn't guarding an empty house.

After a few minutes of thinking it over, I decided it was important for Mickey to know I was there. She answered the door when I rang. I explained I was going to be out front watching her door. She thought it was better for me to stay inside until first light. When she told me she wanted to go to church the next morning, I insisted we telephone Red and get him to help out.

Chapter Six

*Deliberate attacks are fully coordinated
operations that employ all assets against the
enemy's defense.*

----Combat Leader's Field Guide

Sunday May 24, 1943

Mountain folk keep early hours. Believing that I needed to do
the same, I was up well before dawn, sitting in the Model-A parked
across the street, watching Mickey's house. I had arranged with Red
that we would escort Mickey to a church service. I didn't expect her
to be up for several hours because we had been up most of the night
talking about what we needed to do. As for Red, we'd be lucky if
he got here before the service started.

I waited. The first sign of life was the attendant at the service
station, coming out of his room in the back and going around to the
front to open up. About a half an hour after that, there was activity
at the country store beside the filling station. The grocery clerk,
Travis, showed up on a bicycle and went into the store. I could see
his shadow on the front window, passing back and forth. I knew the
first thing Travis did was to make a pot of coffee. I got out of the A
in the hope of cornering a cup of java.

Travis was just pouring himself a cup when I came through the
door. He had some kind of problem with my name. So, his offer
came out, "Cuppa jowa, Hawie?" It sounded like the way Doll Baby
talked, used to talk. Dammit, Cotton Jimson. I was fast running out
of friends, about thirty years ahead of schedule. Every friend I made
in basic training got put into one of those terrible swamp graves on
Guadalcanal.

Thank God for Red, for Mickey and Buck. I didn't have to
worry about them. They were home for the duration. On the other
hand, I needed to get back to my already dead attitude. With who
knows how many more Guadalcanals I would endure, what were
the odds I'd get through them all? With my mug of coffee in hand,
I returned to my observation post. Just as I got so down I was ready

to take poison and die, I saw Mickey come out of her house and go into the store. A minute later, she came over and got into the passenger seat with a mug of coffee.

"What's the last word you had from Buck?" I asked.

"I got a card. It said he was loose in the wide, wide world and would let me know if he settled someplace. Probably not soon."

"How can we get you out from under this, Mickey? We can't follow you around for long. I'm going back on active duty soon."

"Like I said last night, maybe you and Red could help me get rid of Sonny and Anders."

A few minutes later Red showed up, and we were soon ready to go. Red popped into the rumble seat and off we went with the usual clatter of the A's hard-working engine.

The church Mickey had her heart set on was one of the largest buildings in town. It was near Capitol Square and called Christ Church. I asked Mickey, "How often have you been to this church?" With some show of surprise, she said, "Never." Naturally, the next question I asked was, "How about some other church in Raleigh?" No, she hadn't been to any. Before he left, Buck took up her weekends, and he didn't go to church.

The church wasn't crowded when we came in, and we took seats down front. We sat quietly, listening to a medley of hymns played on the organ. Eventually, the congregation was assembled and the service began in earnest. Idly looking to the back of the church, I noticed Sonny and Anders sitting in the pew closest to the door. I pointed them out to Red and whispered to him to go outside and wait for us to come out, to get in behind Sonny and Anders and make sure they don't do us any mischief.

Sonny and Anders must have been watching us react to their presence. The moment Red started down the aisle, they were out the door. Red kept going, but I wasn't happy with this turn of events. I told Mickey to stay where she was and went down the aisle myself. Coming out onto the steps, I noticed Red sitting on the bottom step. As I approached him, I saw he was nursing his head.

"What happened?" I asked him.

"These guys know how to work together. When I came out, the first thing I saw was Sonny holding a sawed-off shillelagh. I had my eye on that and didn't see Anders behind me. He planted one behind my ear, and I went down but not out. I watched them casually walk off, no hurry. These guys might be too good for us, Holly."

"Did you see where they went?"

"Yeah, around behind the church. Probably had some vehicle back there. I guess they're gone by now."

"We've learned a good lesson. We know now that we need to figure out a trap that will work against these booze-runners."

"I'll leave that to you, Sergeant. Let's get Mickey."

We went to the same diner Mickey and Buck had taken me to before, Brownie's railroad dining car.

After we had dealt with our appetites, I started telling them about Leroy's execution. Yes, it wasn't a pleasant lunchtime topic, but it had just happened. I hadn't gotten over it yet.

Red looked eager to hear about it. "What was that like, the electric chair?"

"As bad as anything I saw on Guadalcanal. The odd thing about it is that Leroy told me how awful it could be, then what happened to him was even worse."

Red had a thoughtful expression on his face as he said, "I don't think he deserved all that, but he certainly deserved something. He murdered two people and tried to kill you."

I could see that Mickey wasn't happy to be hearing all this conversation about executions and murders and decided to change the subject.

Before I could do it, Red continued with "It's easy to believe he killed Lana in an out-of-control fit of rage. But why did he hunt down and murder Doll Baby? Nobody was listening to anything Doll Baby had to say, supposing he did know something."

Mickey began tapping her finger on the table. 'Why do the police think he had anything to do with that?"

I decided to take charge of this one, "Everything about it was the same as Lana. Had to be the same man."

Red concluded with, "I guess he deserved what he got. We can't know how much he suffered. Or maybe he never felt anything after that first time."

For some reason I couldn't explain, Mickey was out of touch. Her eyes kind of glazed over. She was like soldiers in a landing craft heading for a beachhead. Overly distracted, staring into space. Shallow breathing or not breathing at all. Remembering all the things you're going to miss if you're killed. Of course, death is final. That's the one really good thing about it. A man steps on a mine and is blown apart. I'm not sure he even experiences any pain. Quickly, he is no more. No pain. No memories. No missing his daughter's wedding. Just gone.

When I looked back again at Mickey, I saw some signs of life stirring.

Abruptly, she flashed a smile at me and said, "Let's get the hell out of here."

And we did.

When we got back to Mickey's house, we found that Sonny and Anders had gotten the jump on us again. The entire place was a shambles. Sofas, chairs, and mattresses were ripped open. Drawers were emptied onto the floor. Even the contents of the kitchen icebox were poured out onto the floor.

Mickey was oblivious to all this. She yelled out, "Joe." She ran through the house and out the back door. Moments later, she was back, exclaiming "Oh! Tabbycattums!" Finally, she went out on the porch and flopped down on the steps.

"Were these tabbynappers? Am I going to find a ransom note?"

"No, Mickey. It was Sonny and Anders, all right." I said.

With some resignation coming into her voice, Mickey said, "How do you know?"

Red broke in with, "They're the buckeroos we're looking for. And, wait and see, when we find them, they'll be some tattered and tore-up."

"Do you think they killed him, Red?" I asked.

"Nope, how could they? But they would certainly have had to contain him somehow. Being who they are, they might want some revenge for whatever he did to them."

I went out back and started looking around. Not finding anything there, I went out front, where Mickey was sitting in the sun.

I walked past her, seeking the shade of the only tree on the property. It had gotten extremely hot for the time of year. In the nineties, I'd say.

Then, I noticed something odd in the tar road. There were two parallel lines going off down the road, starting from the next door driveway. I walked over to the place where the marks began, saw a flat circle in the dirt, and remembered seeing a big red oil drum that someone had been using as a trash can.

I walked down the block following the marks left in the soft, hot tar. The road was flat, with a slight downward grade and no camber. About a block away from Mickey's, it bent to the left in front of a big open field. Already from that distance I could see the red drum out in the middle of this field. I walked to the drum, knelt down and tapped its sides a few times. No response.

I didn't dare open that drum. If the cat was inside, he'd take off in such a panic we'd never see it again.

So I rolled the drum back up the hill. Mickey was still sitting on the porch and looked up when she heard the rumble-rumble of the drum on the road. I rolled the drum up to her yard.

"STOP!" she yelled.

She came rushing over and we righted the drum and pried off the lid. It was half-full of garbage, and we couldn't see any sign of a cat inside, and the giant Joe shouldn't be hard to find inside a barrel. We tipped over the barrel and poured the garbage out onto the grass. When we got near the bottom, a mass of hair soaked with rotten juices and covered with filth, slid out onto the other garbage.

"Tabbycattums!" yelled Mickey, and she reached down to pick up the cat. The moment the stupefied cat felt her touch, he jumped twelve feet laterally and fell over. Stood up and ran in a circle twice, fell over again and was still.

I wasn't sure whether the cat was dizzy from all that rolling or drunk on the fumes of garbage it had been tumbling around in.

"Tabbycattums," screamed Mickey, She ran and picked him up, ignoring the filth.

How about that, love is not only blind, it has no sense of smell.

§

Red and I had a war-room session sitting in the swing on Mickey's front porch. Red started off with, "Here's the way it is, Sergeant. You get me within a few feet of either or both of these booze-geezers, and I'll take 'em down. But I've no idea how to find or get close to 'em. That's your department."

"Okay. Here's where I empty my sack and show what I got." I explained to them that I had spent the early hours this morning thinking about this situation. I worked up some ideas and what has happened this morning has proven them out. I asked myself, where are these two guys? Or, better, how do they know what's happening here? They aren't watching from up close. I was sitting here from before dawn this morning waiting for them to show up. They didn't come, and yet they were in the church. How? It's simple, really. One of them had to be sitting in a car somewhere around Five Points. The other was sitting in another car, probably out around Wake Forest Road. They were covering the two ends of Whitaker Mill Road, watching which way we were going.

Red seemed to ponder these ideas and then asked, "How do they communicate with each other?"

"Good question. I assume the same way they do in the middle of the night, running booze through the Blue Ridge Mountains. I imagine they've got two-way radios of some kind. Similar to walkie-talkies, but much longer range, would be my guess. They've got big needs for that in their business."

"How much range is that? A walkie-talkie I mean."

"Depending on conditions, up to a couple of miles," I told him.

Red pondered again. "Okay, let's say that's what they're doing. What do we do, now that we know that?"

"You're going to have to trust me on one big issue. Are you up to doing that?"

"Sure, what's the big issue?"

"They may or may not be armed, but I don't think that's how they plan to deal with us. Remember the shillelagh. Do you buy it?"

"Sure."

"Okay, then my plan is to draw them in here where the two of us can take 'em out, one on one."

"I'll take one and one-half. You're still not up to full strength."

"Thanks for your support, Red. I'll take the one-half. Here's the plan. I'm going to wear some of Buck's clothes and go down the railroad tracks to the train station. Give me an hour to get there. Then, you and Mickey come down there in the Model-A to pick me up. To be sure they don't miss me, I'll ride in the rumble seat on the way home. Once I'm here in the house, the mouse trap's almost ready. The question is, how do we spring the trap?

"When they move in, they'll do what we did. One will go out back to catch Buck trying to get away. Therefore, when you get out of the A, you circle around to the filling station across the street. As soon as you see one of them approach the house, you come in behind him and I'll be just inside the front door."

Red said, "The one in the back, what about Joe?"

"I asked Mickey about him, and she says he thinks he's still in the barrel. She says whenever he falls asleep, he dreams about the barrel and his legs start to tremble and jerk like he's trying to run. She's keeping him in her bedroom until he gets over it."

"You think the other one will just come to the front door?" Red said.

"I do. These guys are very simple and direct. And dangerous. Don't forget that part. They are dangerous. Remember how they took you at the church."

"Okay, Sergeant, Get dressed and get a move on. We'll be watching the clock."

We did it just the way Red and I discussed. I rode back from the train station in my Buck disguise, with one of his caps pulled down over my eyes, wearing one of his more flamboyant suits. Hey, there is nothing subtle about Sonny and Anders, remember? Two hours after I had laid out the plan to Red, we were back with the bait in the house and the trap set.

Now all we had to do was wait.

§

A knock came at the door. Mickey opened it wide and I saw a man with his hair in a brush cut that gave his face a shape matching the rest of him, a square and squat hombre. It was Anders. He was wearing a short sleeved shirt and bandages were clearly visible on both of his arms, as well as a patch on his neck.

Before Anders got a chance to say a word, Red slammed into him from behind, knocking him to the floor. Unfortunately, Mickey was standing directly in front of Anders and she ended up on the bottom, with her face shoved in between the zippers of Anders' jacket.

"Ummphhff," said Mickey. "Muummhhff."

Red had his knee in Anders' back and he shouted at me, "Check him for weapons."

I rushed to Anders, leaned over and reached around him trying to search the pockets and lining of his jacket. Anders managed to lift himself enough in his struggles that Mickey's head almost popped free.

"Leggo my knockers," said a muffled voice.

I suddenly realized I may have gotten inside the wrong lining. "Sorry, Mic," I said, removing my hands.

To Red, I said, "Pin back his arms and lift him so I can search him."

Red did as I suggested, enabling me to check him for weapons. I found a 32 caliber pistol in his jacket pocket, a pocket knife in his pants pocket, and a sawed-off shillelagh stuck down inside his belt.

"All right, Red, I've got his stuff. You can let him up."

When Red released him, Anders rolled off of Mickey.

She got up and began immediately to shove and punch us both. "Is this the help you're gonna give me, knock me down, feel me up, and try to suffocate me?"

"Sorry, Mickey," said Red. "Do you want me to beat on Anders to make it up to you?"

"No! I don't want you to beat on him. Not yet, anyway."

Turning to Anders, she said, pointing at Red. "Look at the mug on this gent. If you want to start looking like he does, then give me some trouble and we'll see. Now, here's how it's gonna be. You're gonna call Sonny to come over. As soon as he's here, I'm going to make you a proposition."

I looked at Mickey. She had added something new. All I could do, I suppose, was go along. This was her show, after all.

Anders went to the back door, with Red holding onto him, and gave a signal to Sonny. A few minutes later, we were all sitting quietly at Mickey's dining room table. Sonny and Anders were both sitting on their hands. They, along with Red and me, were all looking to Mickey to explain her proposition.

To my total astonishment, the first words from Mickey's lips were: "I'll tell you how to find Buck. You can then go off and do whatever you want. I won't interfere."

Red asked me, "Did you know about this?"

"No," I replied, and turned to Mickey. "What are you doing, Mickey? We can't let them have Buck."

Mickey looked me in the eye and said, "You promised to help me. Now is when I need it, with no questions and no answers, please."

Oddly enough, Sonny didn't seem to be as surprised as I was. He just asked her, "How do I know you won't call Buck and scare him off?"

"I have my reasons."

Sonny said, "I think we may have a deal."

I looked at Red, whose face expressed complete dismay.

"If you do this, Mickey, you'll regret it forever. How can you sell Buck out, just for a little peace of mind?"

Red added, "Mickey, Holly and I can make our own deal with these bozos."

Mickey ignored us and spoke only to Sonny, "The deal is this. I tell you about Buck, and you disappear. You never bother Ida or me again. You leave the rest of my family alone. Do you accept this deal, Sonny?"

"I do," replied Sonny.

"Do you accept this deal, Anders?"

"I do," replied Anders.

Sonny asked Mickey. "Okay, what's next?"

"Red will take your weapons to the post box a block down Whitaker Mill Road and leave them there on top of the box. I'll give you the information as soon as he leaves, and you can follow along and get your weapons. What you do after that is no concern of mine. Just don't come back here."

They agreed. Red collected their assorted arms and other weapons and left.

Mickey said, "Buck is in Winston-Salem. I don't know where he's staying, but he hangs out at the pool room across the street from the Rialto Movie Theatre. That's all I know and all you need to know."

Well, there it was. She sold out her brother and sent the boozer twins on their way. Whatever her reasons were, I'm sure it wasn't about Joe, the Tabby, or whatever else appeared on the surface at this moment. She had always looked out for Buck. The only way I could think of to explain it was that she was trying to look out for the rest of her family.

And here I was just this morning, listing Buck among my friends who were not in harm's way.

§

Red and I went out to his motorcycle where we sat down on the grass to come up with a plan.

Red said, "We don't both need to go. That's a long way on the back of a motorcycle."

"Yeah, you don't need to go, but I do. While we were waiting for the exchange to happen, I worked out a plan to put Buck in a safe place. I'll tell you about it on the way."

"Wait a minute," said Red. "I got a better idea. Let me call my mechanic and get a couple of things done to my plane. It needs some minor work. Even if he needs an hour, we can still beat them to Winston-Salem."

"Hey, the plane. Sure, that's it." I was happy for a moment. Then, I thought, "Hold up, there. I've never flown before, and I don't know if I want to start in a plane you gotta twist somebody's arm to fix in a hurry just before we take off."

"No, my brave Medal of Honor winner, it's nothing like that. It's just routine stuff. Let's find a phone. Or, let's go back in and use Mickey's phone."

We went back into Mickey's house, and Red called his mechanic.

I made a call of my own to someone I knew in Norfolk, Virginia. He was a man of my father's generation. They had known one another when my father was having his youthful adventures building railroads out west. Later, this fellow went into the US Navy in 1910 and retired a Captain. When the war started, he volunteered for the Merchant Navy after the US Navy turned him down. So now he was out there in the Atlantic getting Liberty Ships torpedoed out from under him. We were definitely in luck because he was home.

"Cap," I used the nickname my father used, "I got a volunteer to help you fight your personal war with the Nazis. Can you use a good man?"

"Kid, he doesn't have to be a good man. If he's got at least one leg and one eye, I'll take him. And, if he can cook, I'll drop the requirement for one leg. We can rig up the galley so he can cook sitting down."

"Cap, this guy'd be a perfect cook, if you don't mind living on hot dogs and ice cream sodas."

"Bring him in with his bags packed. We're sailing in a few days from Newport News. You realize I was joking about the physical requirements. There's better than a fifty-fifty chance we'll be sunk every time we go on one of these pleasure cruises. Your man has to be able to make it to a life boat in a hurry and swim like a dolphin if he has to."

"No problem. The guy I'm bringing is very fit. He'll be there tomorrow. One more thing, Cap. Thanks for your help in this matter. It's life or death. My father always spoke highly of you as one of the best men he ever knew. God bless you, and good luck to you in those cold waters of the North Atlantic."

An hour later, Red and I were sitting in a J-3 Piper Cub on a grass airfield north of Raleigh. The plane was a fore and aft two-seater. He was sitting directly behind me studying a map and I was looking at the instrument panel.

"What're you looking for, Red?"

"I've found it already. There's a highway we can follow most of the way to High Point. Then, when we get there, we fly due north to the airport at Winston-Salem.

"If you say so. Are you sure the glue and wire will hold this thing together that long? And how come you're sitting in the back where you can't see the instrument panel?"

Red handed me a pair of earphones and microphone over the seat, saying, "Put these on and speak into the mike from now on. As soon as I rev the engine, we won't be able to hear each other. I don't need to see the instruments. I've seen them before. If I want to know something, I'll just ask you to move your head out of the way."

"What instruments? What are these, anyway?"

"The dial on the left is the airspeed and the one in the center of that is the engine revolutions. To the right of that dial is the altimeter with the rate of altitude change in the lower half. The dial on the right is your basic compass, marked off in degrees from 0 to 359. The little ball-bearing above the altimeter is the turn and bank indicator."

"How does that work?" I asked. "It looks like it's only a little ball bearing."

"We have to bank left or bank right to make turns because the drag on the low wing is what makes the airplane turn in that direction. If we're banking to the left and that little gizmo is all the way to the right, that means we're skidding on the air and not biting into it enough to get a good turn. If it's all the way to the left, that means we're banking too steeply and are falling into the turn. In that case we need to lift the nose and increase our speed. Did you get that?"

"No. Did you say a few minutes ago that the radio doesn't work? How can you fly the plane without a radio?"

Red laughed and said, "Holly, the radio's got nothing to do with flying the plane. Put on your earphones, I'm going to rev the engine."

Red revved the engine up twice, holding it each time for 20 or 30 seconds.

I waited until he was done with that and asked him, "Red, how can you fly the plane without a radio?"

"I have a radio, Holly. I just use it twice. Once, to request permission to take off. Once, to request permission to land. That's all.

Then, he started to taxi the plane across the grass field. As we went along, he kept veering one way and then another. I leaned over the seat and shouted at him, but he just pointed to his mike. "Why are you dodging all over the field?" I said into the mike.

Over the earphones, I heard him reply, "I can't see straight ahead as long as the tail is down. So I have to check out the side that the way ahead is clear."

Out of the corner of my eye, I noticed movement beside my seat and saw that Red's feet were operating pedals there.

Soon, I heard him say, "This is Piper Bravo Easy two three niner requesting takeoff."

I heard a voice in my earphone answer, "Go ahead."

"By the way, don't touch the stick that's in front of you. I mean, whatever you do, don't touch that, ok?"

"Got it."

Suddenly the engine revved way up, and we started moving forward, the plane rising and falling slightly on its springs. Before long, the tail came up, and I could see straight ahead of the plane for the first time. It bounced a few times on the grass and, when the airspeed got up to about 50 miles an hour, it lifted off the grass. A few moments after it lifted, the plane shifted around sideways about twenty degrees to the left. "What happened, Red? Why did we turn?"

"We didn't turn. The wind shifted to come from the left when we got a few feet off the ground. I adjusted so the propeller compensates for the wind, and we keep flying straight, in the direction we want to go."

We were soon flying along at 3000 feet, and I was amazed at the view. There were cars like beetles scooting along roads, farmers plowing their fields, their wives hanging the wash or weeding their cabbage patch.

"Hey, Red, now I know what those Japs saw looking down at Henderson Field. I'm amazed they ever missed. They should have been able to kill us all."

I felt like an angel or god looking down on the world, on the earthbound world. The soaring of the aircraft brought a feeling of elation. In an odd way, I felt close to the people down below, closer than I had felt toward anyone in a long time, since before Guadalcanal.

After we had been at it for an hour, I asked Red, "Are you sure we're going to beat them there? We're following the same highway they're taking."

"Well, looking over your shoulder, I see our airspeed is 70 mph. Since we have a tailwind of maybe 15 knots, that means we're doing above 90 mph groundspeed. Take that with the fact that although we are guided by the highway, we aren't following it exactly. We're flying straight whereas the highway is crooked. They'll probably have to drive at least fifty miles more than we fly."

"Great, Red. When will we get there?"

"About ten minutes."

Red had it right. We circled over a field just south of Winston-Salem. Red cut the engine on the downwind leg. He told me on the intercom that we were too high. Then, as we were coming in on the final approach, the plane suddenly turned sideways. I yelled at Red, "What happened? Have you lost control?"

"No," Red replied. "This is a side slip. We need to lose altitude in a big hurry without picking up airspeed. We're not actually flying right now; we're in a controlled fall."

He was right about losing altitude in hurry. When we started falling, the runway was like 500 feet below us, right below us. Now it was rushing up at us fast. It seemed we were coming straight down. Falling is right. Just when I was going to ask Red if it would be okay for me to jump out, the plane suddenly swung back around, the nose dipped forward a moment, then pulled up and we touched down in a three-point landing as smooth and soft as a baby's cheek.

§

Red and I were soon in downtown Winston-Salem. We found the Rialto Theatre without delay and went into the pool room across the street.

From there on, it all became routine. Buck was there and, when he saw me, he knew the game was up. I explained to him that he was like a man joining the French Foreign Legion, except in his case it was the US Merchant Marines. He agreed to everything because he knew his good luck had run out. Buck was a difficult guy in many ways, but he could be reasonable when he had his back up against the wall.

In the end, the only things Buck seemed unable to understand was the fact that Mickey had betrayed him.

"Tell me word for word what she said," he asked.

I wanted to explain it to him, but I didn't understand it myself.

"What can I say, Buck. She didn't say anything except that we had promised to support her, no questions asked, and that she wanted them to leave her family alone."

"So you're telling me the basic deal was a trade of my life for the worthless creeps in my family?"

"That's my take on it, yeah. You go along with that, Red?"

164

"Yeah. Too bad, I was eager to apply some boxology to the situation."

I told Red to get on with it before Cap's ship put to sea. Soon, he and Buck left for the airport to fly to Newport News.

After Red and Buck were gone, I walked to the Greyhound Bus terminal. I noticed that downtown Winston-Salem was a lot like downtown Durham. They were both factory towns built by the Duke and Reynolds tobacco empires. I walked through block after block of single-story, gray, windowless buildings covering both sides of the street.

When I got to the station, I checked on buses to Raleigh and noticed there was a bus to Salem, the town associated with the Moravian Church. Having just walked through the source of all that Reynolds' wealth, I wondered if that accounted for the continued presence into modern times of the Moravian Church, which had given him his original grant of property to build his first factory.

Then, I remembered Mose telling me that Jerome was a part of that church, giving his Sermon on the Mount, and that LaBelle wanted me to talk with him. I didn't see the point of it, but I couldn't think of any reason not to go, given that I was only a couple of miles away. I took that bus.

On the way to Salem, I thought about Jerome. When I was fourteen, I experienced the presence of magic, though it certainly did not seem magical at the time. The neighbor Price kept his truck loaded with ice and fish for his deliveries. At night when it was parked in front of LaBelle's, the melting ice dribbled and drabbled out onto the street, collecting on the curb of the down-hill side of the street and then ran the length of the block to a drain at the far corner. Unfortunately, the water reeked of the odor of dead fish which was why there was a neighborhood feud over it.

The block I had to walk to get home lay in the direction of the flow, and as I walked along I began to be bothered by the odor. In the dim light, I could see the silhouette of the truck that had to be there. I passed it, not holding my nose, but holding my breath. I noticed the driver had left a tow sack lying behind the truck along the curb. He had never done that before. But, it wasn't any of my business.

I walked along thinking of the contents of the tow sack. Many times, I had seen Price come out of his place, get into his truck from that side, back up two or three feet with his steering wheel cranked over toward the curb to bring his front wheels out, then crank his front wheel around toward the street and slowly move forward up the hill. I realized he was not going to see the tow sack and would simply back right over it. Probably that wouldn't matter. But, what was in the tow sack? Maybe something of value would be crushed.

I walked back to examine the tow sack. As I came up to it, I realized that it had been there quite a while, soaking up that juice draining from the truck. It was mighty ripe. One end of the sack was right up against the curbside wheel of the truck. I got down on my knees, away from the drippings and looked up under the truck. I saw that there was a head nestled into the hollow formed by the truck wheel and the curb. I drew back so quick I bumped my head on the rear bumper of the truck.

I rubbed the knot on my head a couple of moments, then crawled all the way under the truck, feeling my hands and knees getting wet from the fish water. I got close enough to see the face. It was Jerome Blue.

Mister Price was a man who got up and out early in the morning and might come at any moment. Somehow, it didn't cross my mind that I could just remain there and tell him about Jerome. I felt a great anxiety about getting Jerome out from under the truck before he got run over.

I didn't have any idea at what hour LaBelle started her days, but I felt sure I could get her up to help out with Jerome. I rushed across her yard, for once empty of sheets, ducking under the lines, and knocked at LaBelle's front door. When there was no answer, I went around to her bedroom and knocked on the boards. I heard some muffled sounds, went back to the front door and knocked again. Soon, the door opened and LaBelle stood before me dressed in a pair of men's long johns, the ones with the buttons up the front and the big, buttoned-up flap in the back.

"Come quick, Tatie, Jerome's about dead in the gutter." Having said this, I turned and ran back toward the street. When I got back to the street, I turned and was surprised to see LaBelle right behind me, with her long johns and bare feet. I pointed out Jerome in the gutter. In the better light, I could see that there was no tow sack. It was just an old coat he had on.

LaBelle and I grabbed his legs and pulled hard enough to drag Jerome a couple of feet. She said, "Lift him onto the sidewalk."

I went up to Jerome's head, stooping under the truck to get my hands under his arms. I lifted him up to a half sitting position, but when LaBelle lifted his feet, Jerome melted away from my grip and though I tried to catch him, he kept slithering this way and that, until his head thumped as it hit the street. I thought, "We've killed him."

LaBelle said, "Lift him up again."

I could hardly believe it, but exactly the same thing happened the second time we lifted him. Poor Jerome got another thump on the head.

"Tatie, I think I killed him," I said.

LaBelle stood up straight and said, "You can't kill a drunk that easy." She paused there for a moment and changed her position to be alongside Jerome and said, "Roll 'im."

She bent over and got a grip under his thighs. I grabbed his arm and his belt and we lifted him away from the curb and shoved and rolled him all at the same time. After several tries we managed to get him rolled up onto the sidewalk. He certainly reeked, and not just of dead fish.

"Leave him. Drunk fool can look after himself," said LaBelle. She turned and went back toward her house.

I looked at Jerome lying there and realized there was not another thing I could do for him. I went home to bed.

I found out about the miracle two months later when LaBelle told me that Jerome had quit drinking and was enrolled at a Baptist college on a tuition scholarship, intending to study for the ministry.

That was the magic, that amazing change in Jerome.

When the bus arrived in Salem, I found something completely different from the factory town of Winston. It was both a town and a Moravian religious community. There was the look of a 1750 colonial town that was centered on a large, open square where the whole town could gather for a meeting.

Along the borders of the square were blacksmith shops with axles and other heavy pieces of metal scattered around in front of each shop and out into the square.

The stores around the square were open markets, tables piled with goods under the shade of tin roofs.

I stopped at a smithy and asked for help from a blacksmith who was busy pounding out a white-hot piece of metal. He asked me, "Did you say Bountiful Blue? Cause if you did, he'll be yonder," pointing to a hill south of town.

§

I went out in that direction and began to notice others going that way. A booming voice began to be heard, first faintly and then louder and louder as I walked along.

"Is our Nation being led by men who have given themselves over to Satan? They have built a war machine to destroy one half of the world to save the other half."

As I approached, I saw that people in the crowd were all dressed in plain style, black homespun clothes with no adornments whatever. Suits worn by the men were cut in straight lines with horn buttons and no pockets. The women wore black, long-sleeved dresses coming down to their ankles. I arrived directly in front of Bountiful, perhaps fifty feet away.

I recognized Jerome, though he was a changed man. He was of medium build, maybe five foot eight. His outstanding new feature, one that made his face appear to be two feet long, was his large hair, prematurely gray, that stood up straight as the Cliffs of Dover.

I could tell he saw me. For several minutes as he spoke he glanced back and forth between me and his congregation.

"What about the heroes of this war? Are they righteous? Or, are they mass-produced like the tanks and planes? Let me tell you about a young man from Raleigh. Sergeant Rollins.

"As it happens, I knew this man when he was a boy, a few years younger than I was. He lived next door to my grandmother, and we were friends and played together at her house. I tell you this boy was meek and kind, and she loved him. But, how can he be righteous as a soldier killing his enemies?

"What he did was done in obedience to God, not to honor the lust for power of the men in Washington. God's voice spoke to his heart, and he answered that call. In the face of an invincible enemy, God directed Sergeant Rollin's hand, just as he directed David's hand when he slew Goliath. God made Sergeant Rollins of the same

168

earth from which he created us all and turned him into the Good Mud of a Faithful Servant. And now as he returns from that battlefield, God says to him, Thank you, Mud! You have shown yourself to be a righteous man, worthy to have your name placed beside the name of David."

I was stunned by Bountiful's remarks. His words made me aware of the guilt embedded in my heart, a heavy and unshakable guilt. Maybe if Doc Windsor hadn't introduced me to the demon, I might have been gratified by what Jerome had to say about me.

When the sermon was finally over, I approached him as he spoke to a group of disciples. When I said his name, he turned to me, "Boy Moon, all raised up to a man."

"Thanks for not putting me on your list of war criminals," I said.

"You don't deserve that, Moon. Here's somebody you'll remember." The Reverend Bountiful Blue turned and said, "Sudie, come over her. You, too, Sweetheart."

Two young women separated themselves from the group and approached. Bountiful said, "Moon, you remember Little Sudie, of course. And this is my sister who has changed so much you may not know her."

"In fact, LaBelle asked me to come here, Jerome, to find out if you have any information about your sister, Lana."

"Of course. What information does she want?"

"About what happened to her, you know."

Bountiful turned to the young woman with Sudie and said, "Well, Holly, ask her yourself. This is Lana, my only sister. Get the information from her."

I turned to the woman standing beside Little Sudie. Although I did then recognize her, I couldn't help but ask anyway, "Lana Blue?"

"Yes," she replied. "What does Granbelle want to know?"

I wouldn't say I was weak in the knees. Maybe, it was just that my blood pressure dropped faster than the stock market on Black Monday.

"Lana, I need to sit down, and we need to talk. How we need to talk. Is there someplace we can do that?"

"Follow me," she said. I followed her around the hill where there was a cabin in a clump of trees. There was a wooden bench against the wall. We headed for that without talking until we were seated.

"Did you know that everyone in Raleigh thinks you're dead?"

"Who's been thinking that?" Lana said.

"Your grandmother, the police, myself, everyone has been thinking that. A woman was murdered near your cabin on Slippery Rock Creek a few months ago. Everyone thought it was you."

"Who was murdered?"

"Marla Brown."

"Marla, are you sure?"

"Yes, I am. There's no other possibility."

Lana burst into tears. "I was so afraid something might happen to her. Who did it?"

"Leroy Struthers was tried for the murder and condemned to death."

I had to wait until Lana got better control of herself to continue. In a few minutes the first wave of grief passed.

She said, "Leroy Struthers was acting crazy. He scared me sometimes because he's not much ahead of Cotton in the brains department. He was jealous. I told Marla I needed to come here to get away from all that and find some peace and quiet."

"What did he do that frightened you?"

"He would come in the middle of the night and throw rocks at the cabin door. Throw them hard. Those rocks banging against the door would wake us up. Then he would yell and run off. And one night after the store closed, he beat her up. Maybe, I should say they had a fight. I'm not sure who won it. That was just before I left."

"Why was he jealous?"

"Marla's one big problem was the way she used men. She liked having them around and liked getting presents."

"When did you come down here?"

"At least three months ago. It's hard to say because time doesn't mean nothin' here. You forget about it."

Lana's head sank down onto her chest. She looked to be on the verge of tears again. I sat quietly, studying her and thinking over the whole situation. After a few minutes she looked up and asked, "What's happening now? How is Granbelle taking it?"

"Don't you get any news here? Don't you read a newspaper now and then?"

"Are you kidding? This community cut itself off from the outside world two hundred years ago. They send things out but nothing comes in. My brother travels and brings back news sometimes. But he goes to churches in Greensboro and Durham, not Raleigh."

"Didn't you get any letters from friends or relatives?"

"Marla was the only friend who knew where I was. Why did they think I was killed, too? Do they think he buried me someplace or threw me in the river?"

"No, they made a mistake when they identified Marla's body. They thought it was you."

"Why'd they think that?"

"Her face was bashed in with an iron bar." I was planning to say more but saw the tears welling up in her eyes again and stopped there.

She stayed for several minutes with her head lowered again, looking at nothing. Then she said, "I understand. She and I made an effort to look alike. We are the same size and wear the same clothes. Her cheek bones and lips are different from mine. But if her face was bashed in, I can see why someone might make that mistake." She hesitated a moment or two. "What now?"

"I'm not sure. Leroy was convicted of murdering you and sentenced to the chair."

Lana continued her pensive mood for several minutes. "What about Marla? What do they think happened to her?"

"The police think she ran away, out of fear of Leroy. Really, they do have it all completely backwards, since that's what you did."

"I loved Marla Brown. I even preferred her ways over my own. She was everything I wanted to be and didn't know how. People in my family judged her a bad person. She did have her craziness and too many boyfriends. But I liked the way she was living her life in a way I couldn't. I needed to break free of my family. They were stuck in their lives like they were anchored in cement."

She sat quite still for several long moments. "I know there's defense work for women out in California, making airplanes. Welding and driving tractors. That's for me. I want to have my own place to live and do what I want."

"Listen, Lana, one thing is for sure. You must go see Granbelle Blue before you do anything else." She was going to do that if I had to drag her to Raleigh myself.

"Lana, another thing I'd like to clear up. Did you ever go back to your place on Slippery Rock Creek after coming over to stay with your brother?"

"Yes, I did. I didn't bring many things with me because I wasn't planning to stay long. When I changed my mind, I asked Jerome to drive me over in his car. He doesn't drive it much, so he had enough ration stamps to cover the trip."

"Did you see anybody while you were there?"

"Yes, I saw Cotton. I passed his place and he was there. So, I stopped in to see him."

"How do you manage to communicate with him? I tried and got nowhere."

"It depends on how excited he is. When he's worked up, he gets foggy. When he's peaceful, he can carry on a conversation about everyday things."

"When I spoke with him, he just kept yelling muddy. I couldn't get past that."

"Muddy is his way of saying Marla. He has trouble with her name."

"You mean the whole time I was trying to get him to say something about your death, he was telling me it was Marla?"

"He knew I wasn't dead. I said good-by to him when I left. He must have known Marla was there. She gave him coffee in the morning. Holly, the more I think about it, the more surprising it is to me that Leroy killed Marla. She could handle him. If I was going to pick somebody who might have killed her, I would have picked the white man she was involved with."

"No, Lana, it wasn't him. That was thoroughly checked out and he couldn't possibly have done it."

Another few minutes passed, and I asked Lana, "Are you feeling a bit chilly? I think there's a storm coming in."

"No, I'm all right. I've been meaning to ask you. How is Ida?"

"Do you know Ida?"

"No, I've heard about her."

"What have you heard about her?"

"Oh, you don't realize how your connection to Granbelle affects my whole family."

"I don't understand."

"I only wish Marla had fallen for you instead of that other guy. She liked older men, and you would have been perfect for her. And she'd still be alive."

Something didn't jell about this wish of hers. "I don't follow what you're saying. Leroy was only about twenty-four and the Sergeant is twenty-three."

"She wasn't interested in either one of them."

"Who was she interested in?"

"I couldn't describe him. I only saw him once, just for a minute. But, I do remember Marla saying he was a friend of yours."

Could she be talking about Red? I didn't know anybody else who went down to that place and who knew Marla.

Lana continued, "I remember she had a movie nickname for him, like she did for everybody. Who was that one in the rocket ship? What was his name?"

"Lana, you don't mean *Flash Gordon*, do you?" What the newspapers called Red during his football days. "Do you know Red Carter, a white guy, who came into that place on South Street sometimes?"

"The only white guys I've seen are policemen."

"This Flash Gordon, did he have red hair and a face all beat up, like a box-fighter?"

"I don't picture him that way, but that sounds like him."

She couldn't remember anything more about Flash Gordon, and I was happy to let it drop for the present.

We discussed getting her over to Raleigh to see LaBelle. Bountiful had a commitment to speak at a church in Durham in four days. Maybe he could drive us all to Raleigh and then go by Durham on his way back.

When we put this idea to Jerome, he was delighted at the idea of getting to see his family. He had been an outcast long enough.

§

I waited in Winston-Salem for Jerome and Lana to show up. He went to get his car from storage someplace in Winston. He and Lana were going to pick me up at a filling station on the border of the two towns.

They showed up in a Ford two-door, in one of those odd, off-colors available when Ford first started to deliver colors other than black, back in nineteen-thirty-four. It was a brownish mustard color that would have looked better on a hotdog. The back seat was comfortable, bulky and leathery.

We drove through the downtown sections of Greensboro and Durham. These were towns I had been through many times before, while doing my road work in western North Carolina. We made good time because of the light traffic. Gas rationing kept many cars sitting on cinder blocks in the back or side yards. The stop lights were regulated to favor through traffic on the main highways coming through town.

When we got to Raleigh, we drove past the hospital and turned onto Fontaine Street. I didn't see LaBelle from the street, and I told the others to wait in the car until they saw a signal from me. "She can't see either one of you until we've gotten her prepared for it."

LaBelle was working in her victory garden. I went up to her and helped her to her feet. "Tatie, I've got great news. I found Jerome and he's more than all right. He's back on the right path as a preacher in a religious community in Salem. He wants to see you."

It was obvious that my words had a big effect on her. She took off her bonnet and when I had finished said, "God Bless you, Moon, for finding Jerome and bringing me this news. I've really missed him."

"I also have some news about Lana."

"Did you find her body?"

"Do you remember her friend Marla? The one you thought was using cocaine."

"Of course I do. What are you getting at?"

"Marla was murdered out by the railroad tracks near Slippery Rock Creek."

"When did that happen? Do they know who did it?"

"It happened on February the fourteenth."

"The same day?" She paused and seemed to be confused. "Why was her body never found?"

"It was found. That same day. By the track inspector, who didn't know that Marla was living out there in Lana's shelter."

"Are you saying.....?"

"Yes."

"Marla?"

"Yes, Tatie. Marla was the woman who was murdered. Lana is still alive."

"How could that be? Where's she been all this time? It doesn't make any sense, Moon."

"It does make sense. She was with her brother in Salem and never heard anything about the murder because that community has no radio, no newspaper, and no interest in the outside world. Come with me, Tatie."

I took her right hand in my left, and we walked around the house to a point where the car could be seen. I raised my right hand and waved for Lana and Jerome to come. The moment they stepped from the car, LaBelle squeezed my hand with all her might. All her tough years gave her a powerful grip. I was about to complain, when she released my hand and hurried forward to meet Lana, who had come down from the sidewalk in two jumps and was hurrying to LaBelle. The two women locked in an embrace.

They stood hugging each other for several minutes. Meanwhile, Jerome crossed the yard and waited his turn. When she and Lana did separate, I got a good look at LaBelle's face and got worried. In spite of my precautions, she was looking wobbly on her feet. I grabbed both her arms and braced her against my body. Jerome was ready to give her a hug, but instead, wrapped his arms about her as I had done and helped support her weight.

I was afraid she was going to go down. She turned and looked at me, whispering "Moon." Even her voice sounded like a stranger's, someone scared and lacking confidence, unlike LaBelle, who was never afraid and always confident.

I said to Jerome, "Let's get her over to the porch."

Between the two of us, we managed to get her there. She wasn't able to help all that much. She seemed to me still about ready to go down.

Lana brought a rocking chair down the steps, and we put LaBelle in it. Even sitting down, she was not able to hold herself up and lolled over to one side, with her head hanging on her shoulder. I could feel an increasing anxiety coming over me. "Do you think she's had a stroke?" I asked.

LaBelle lifted her head and said, "Snuff."

"Snuff? You want snuff?" I asked.

"Snuff," she replied.

"What happened to the snuff you had?" I asked her.

"Swallowed," she said and let her head settle back again.

Lana came down the steps with a snuff box in her hand. She surprised me by grabbing LaBelle by the lower lip and pulling it out. She took the box, tilted it over and poured one-half its contents, like she was filling a feed trough. When she was finished, she released LaBelle's lip which popped back into place, showing its usual bulge.

"How's that Granbelle?" Jerome leaned over LaBelle to look in her face and, perhaps, get some idea of how she was doing.

LaBelle's head was hanging down, and she was looking at her apron. She raised her head again until she was looking at Jerome, looking at him like a demented person would, almost without recognition. She slowly turned and looked at Lana in the same way. Her eyes squinted as she stared at Lana. Suddenly, she dropped her face down into her lap and began to wail, a piercing noise, neither a cry of mourning nor of anguish, but of deep, eternal despair.

I was too astonished to react in any way other than to stand looking down at her heaving back and, then to look from Jerome to Lana and back to Jerome again. We were, all of us, as dumbfounded as could be. The forever sound and solid LaBelle Blue seemed to have been hit by a seismic wave with enough power to derail a freight train.

As time passed and LaBelle continued her wailing, the three of us slowly drifted together about ten feet away from her tortured, bent-over form.

I whispered, "I don't think we should disturb her. I've spent the past couple of months on the wildman reservation, and I've noticed that when something like this happens, it is probably going to turn out to the good."

Jerome didn't register a happy thought as he listened, but he didn't protest either.

Lana said, "I don't think I understand what you mean by good, I guess. Because, this looks God-awful bad to me."

Suddenly, the world went silent again. The wailing stopped. The three of us turned to see LaBelle stand up. Obviously, her strength was back.

LaBelle Blue walked toward us, saying, "I drove Tyler away, saying it was his fault. Now, he's dead, and it's too late to make that up. I told Mose not to come back here and blamed him for leaving. You, Jerome, I said I couldn't put up with you, and you had to go, and you went. I told myself, 'Good riddance.' Lana, I chased you away and thought you were wicked."

LaBelle stopped, turned and walked back to the porch. She picked up a tin from the end of the top step, and sat down again in the rocking chair.

"Why did I do all this?"

She spat into the can.

"I was afraid of my church and of my neighbors. I didn't want to look bad to people. I didn't want to be run off. It was all me, me, me."

She spat into the can again.

"Then, my granddaughter rose from the dead. Not in three days, like Jesus. But, in three months. She had to rise from the dead for me to see myself as a stupid fool, as a human fool. Because I am human. I'm not a saint. I don't have any answers. Before, I had answers. Now, I have my dear Moon. I have my grandson, Jerome Blue. And I have a grand-daughter, returned from the dead to bless us and to bring us together. Lana Blue, my baby."

Lana approached LaBelle, saying "Grandma, I wasn't dead."

LaBelle rose from her chair. "I know, Child."

The two of them fell into each others' arms again. This time, they were both sobbing and laughing at the same time. Jerome kept patting me on the back and giving me hugs, until I went up the steps and stood in the corner of the porch where he couldn't get at me. He grabbed Lana and LaBelle instead and hugged them, saying:

"Almighty God! How do we know you? Through your Amazing Grace. You wreck our lives beyond repair and get us listening real hard. And then, with one stroke, you put it all back together again in a way no one but you could have done. You turn our faces to you and purify our hearts. You are the Lord God. We honor and glorify You. We have many Names for You, but we don't know Your Name. You are the One Living God, beyond our ideas and understanding, and we give our thanks to You today for this magnificent healing. We rejoice in the blessing you bestowed upon your daughter, our cherished Granbelle. Amen."

Jerome and Lana helped LaBelle up the steps. She turned to me and said, "Jerome, give your car keys to Moon and, Moon, you go over to the store and bring Mose. He needs to be a part of this."

Jerome tossed me his keys and the three of them went into her home.

I was not even aware of the drive to the store. Then, on the way back with Mose in the car, I was careful breaking the news about Lana to him. For all I knew, he could be even more fragile than LaBelle. But he took it better than she did, not having the load of guilt LaBelle had been carrying around. The moment we stopped, he left the car heading for her front door.

I knew that LaBelle was expecting me to come in with Mose, but was happy to have done for her what I had promised. And more even than that, I was remembering Ida, how she used to come every day to the soda fountain to get change for a twenty. Looking up at the night sky, I said, "Thanks for the memories."

And, in a moment of being restored to my past, my feelings for Ida Patini returned to me, and I realized I loved her and had never stopped loving her. She had somehow been frozen out of my heart like everyone else.

Now, I was going to talk with Red. Then, I was going to find out about where I stood with Ida.

Chapter Seven

*Know human nature, human needs and
emotions; how people respond to stress;
character strengths and weaknesses;
knowledge and skills of your people.*

----Combat Leader's Field Guide

Monday   May 25, 1943

I got out of bed dressed in my khaki underwear, thinking I'd
have a shower before going down to breakfast, when there was a
soft knock on the door. I opened up and found Red standing in the
hall with his head drooping so far forward I couldn't see his face
under the bill of his baseball cap.

He said, "Get ready and meet me downstairs. We got a hard
task to do. I'll tell you about it as we go."

After sixteen months in the service, I was used to taking orders
without question. Five minutes later we were walking side by side,
going somewhere, I didn't know where. And for a block, Red didn't
say.

Finally, I said, "At least tell me where we're going."

"To the Purifying Parlor," he replied, then lapsed again into
silence for another couple of blocks.

But this time I knew he would soon continue. And, he did.

"We got to tell Mickey that Buck's dead."

"What happened? Did you crash your plane?"

"No. I took him, all right, to Newport News. Even to the dock
where Cap's ship was tied up. He went on board, and I left."

Red went silent again for a block as we continued toward Ida's
Purifying Place. He picked up his story, "Back at the airport, I
checked my logs and found I needed some routine maintenance. It
could've waited until I got back. But, I thought, why not look around
Newport News. I asked a mechanic to do the work and went into
town and took a room."

Again, Red stopped and I waited for him to continue as we walked on. "Cap's ship was the Donna Marie. I saw the name watching Buck go aboard her. That next morning I looked at the local paper and there was a big article about a ship blowing up in the channel leading down river to the ocean, a shipping channel. The Donna Marie. Seems Nazi U-boats like to mine that channel because it's narrow. Witnesses say it just blew up. She must have been carrying explosives. Lifted right out of the water and was gone. All hands went down with her."

"I guess Cap got used to thinking he was just gonna take a dunk in cold water. Poor old Cap. Poor old crafty Buck, too. I thought he was too clever to get caught this way."

"Maybe it was just because he was on the run and lost his touch." Red stood looking at me for a minute of silence to ponder the ways of Nazi U-boats. Then, he went to the subject he really wanted to talk about.

"You gotta be the one tells Mickey about it. Okay? You know her better."

"I'll tell her, Red. But, you know, she must be expecting to hear bad news about Buck after turning him over to a couple of killers."

"I know, Holly, but this kind of news is always a surprise, even if you did cause it to happen. For whatever reason she done it, now she has to deal with a dead brother."

By this time, we were standing in front of the building with Ida's big Purified sign. Today was not redemption day. I had a terrible feeling about Buck and about having to talk with Mickey.

Red just stood there studying the door and said, finally, "I'll wait here."

When I went in, I found Mickey vacuuming the parlor. She turned off the machine when she saw me.

"Ida's not in yet, Holly."

"Something's happened to Buck. I've come to talk to you about it."

"They caught up with him. That's it, isn't it?"

"No, this is not about Sonny and Anders. Red took Buck to a freighter anchored in Newport News, captained by my father's friend Cap. I talked Buck into disappearing into the Merchant Navy for the duration."

180

Mickey was starting to look relieved, that somehow the news was not going to turn out as she feared. I knew I'd better get to the point now.

"Cap's ship was sunk, going down with all hands, just after leaving its berth in Newport News. Buck is dead, along with Cap and the rest of the crew."

Mickey stood looking at me without moving. Seconds passed without any reaction from her. I was starting to think it wouldn't be as bad as I feared when, to my complete surprise, she ran to me, threw her arms around my neck, and burst into tears. We stood like that for maybe five minutes. Then, without saying a word, she took me by the hand over to the door and showed me out.

I said to Red, "You called it right. It broke her heart even though she did it."

Red said, "Holly, maybe it broke her heart because she did it."

I looked around the Parlor and had an urgent need to get out of there.

"Red, let's go. I don't want to be here when Ida shows up."

"Sure," he said.

When we were out on the street and walking toward downtown, I said to him, "Remember, I said I'd warn you if I changed my mind about Ida?"

Red stopped cold in the middle of a street we were crossing. "You don't need to go on. I've known all along this day was coming. You know how? Because Ida's never shown any interest in anybody but you. And you're always real quiet when she's around."

The only appropriate thing I could think of to say was, "Red, I think we better get out of the street."

Safely on the sidewalk, he said, "Listen, Sergeant Holly, I'm not in your way. Never have been, worse luck. Invite me to the wedding."

With that, Red turned and walked off.

As I watched him go, I found it impossible to believe he was a murderer. I remembered how spooked he was at Lana's shelter when he thought the murder happened there.

Ida and I went to a moving picture show the next night. As we approached the Ambassador Theatre, we walked past a plain, unmarked door that I remembered was the Negro-only entrance to the Theatre.

The marquee had hundreds of light bulbs in a variety of colors. There was a large, backlit white section where the movie title was displayed in large black letters, *Benny's Big Broadcast*.

The walls inside were covered with crimson cloth and golden light fixtures. The curtain had red glass crystals reflecting patterns of other bright colors. The curtain came up and the movie started. It took me awhile to get into the movie.

Midway through the film, there was a scene between Jack Benny and Eddie (Rochester) Robinson coming after a whole series of scenes where Jack had been acting against Rochester's advice in his treatment of Mary Livingstone. Finally, Jack says, "Well, I think I handled that well, if I do say so myself." Eddie replied, "Yeah! That's why she took our car and went off with the saxophone player."

There was some laughter in the white section and an outburst in the second balcony, the Negro section. After a few moments, the white audience heard the noises coming from above. They stopped laughing and sat listening to a black audience enjoying itself. And, then, a surprising thing happened. In an instant, people in the second balcony suddenly woke up to the situation. The laughers stopped laughing and the chucklers stopped chuckling. The second balcony abruptly went silent.

Both audiences sat in silence for a few minutes as the movie continued, waiting for sounds from across the barrier. And then, the next surprising thing happened. They forgot about each other. The mantle of invisibility settled again, and each audience vanished from the perception of the other.

My nerves began to jump as I sat thinking about this situation. Finally, I turned to Ida and said, "I want to leave." I was hoping she would say, "Of course" or just get up. Instead, she said, "Why?"

"I'll tell you outside," I said as I got to my feet.

When we got outside I tried explaining to Ida what had caused my upset.

"I couldn't stand the wait for another outbreak of laughter."

She had a hard time understanding how laughter could have bothered me so much. After all, laughter is a good thing. She stared at me for a long moment. "What are you talking about?"

"I meant laughter from the second balcony."

Ida hesitated a moment, then asked, "What second balcony?"

"The Negro section," I said.

"What Negro section? Are you all right? You spend too much time thinking about LaBelle and her problems."

There you have it. Segregation works. People become blind to the ones behind the wall of segregation. Don't tell me that in all the times she had come to the principal motion picture theatre of Raleigh that she had never noticed black people waiting in line at the black entrance, only thirty paces away from the white entrance?

I said, "Let's go to the diner on Hillsboro Street and have their special paprika home fries."

"Okay, but I've got to be home early."

"That way, it's not far to walk you home afterwards."

There was a counter running the length of the diner, separating the space into equal parts with a row of stools on our side. We sat down and put in our order.

"Why are you so set against LaBelle?"

Ida's face took on an impatient, drawn-skin look, as she said, "I don't like her coming to my place of business. One evening, she was waiting for me when I left work, and she asked me when Moon was coming home. Why does she call you Moon? No one else does."

"It's just a nickname from childhood; maybe I had a moon-pie face."

The cook was finishing up our home fries, tossing potato chunks into the air, catching them as they came down in a stream, as though they were held together by string.

"What did you tell her?" I asked.

Ida's glare flashed at me again as she said, "What could I tell her? I didn't know anything. I told her I would tell you. So, LaBelle wanted to see you. You have now been told. And I don't like her coming to my place like that. Tell her that in future when she has a message for you, she can send a telegram. While we're talking about this, I don't understand why you put yourself out for this Negro when you wouldn't even write me a letter when I was so worried about you."

"I made a bad mistake not writing to you. I didn't want you to wait for me. After the first few battles we had, I didn't see how I could live through any more. You'd be waiting for nothing."

"You never said that before," Ida spoke slowly, her words evenly spaced.

"I'm not sure I ever figured it out, until I had help from Doc Scott. Ida, it was like an emotional state I got into where I dreaded even to think of it. I avoided the whole subject. That's why I couldn't bring myself to sit down to write you a letter, even a goodbye letter. I'd have had to confront the possibility that I wasn't going to come back to you, and I didn't know how to do that."

The cook put plates before us, and I attacked mine, releasing a pent-up energy. Ida picked at hers. When we had finished, I forked out fifty-five cents, forty-five for the java and spuds and a generous ten cent tip.

Little was said on the walk to her house. When we got to her door, I told her there was a county fair at the State Fair Grounds at Cary and asked if she wanted to go. She said she did, and we made a date to go.

§

When I asked Ida if she'd like to go to the county fair, I warned her about the weather. We were having a week of rain and no getting around it, with the fair only here for one week. But she told me she had wet-weather clothing.

I went to her place on Jones Street right after having eaten an early dinner. That seemed better than the cotton candy and taffy at the Fairgrounds. I rapped on her door.

Ida appeared and as usual managed to surprise me. She was wearing one of those heavy woolen pea coats that, although they are slow to absorb water, will hold as much as a rain barrel. She had on a red and black plaid woolen shirt and black flannel trousers stuffed down into bright yellow, rubber boots. She topped it all off with a scarlet rubber cap shaped like a beret that she pulled down over her hair like a bath-cap.

I decided it was best not to comment on her choices and said, "Would you like to get a meal before we go out to the fairgrounds?"

"No," Ida said "I just ate."

"Let's hitchhike to the fairgrounds," As soon as I said these words, a parade of doubts crossed Ida's face, ending with her telling me it would be all right.

We walked up to Hillsboro Street where I pulled a roll of paper from my back pocket.

"What's that?" said Ida.

"What's getting us to the fairgrounds, double quick."

With that, I unrolled my paper to reveal a hand lettered sign 'FAIRGROUNDS, PLEASE'.

When Ida saw it, her expression lightened up and she said, "As good as a ticket."

And it was. Within five minutes we had a ride with a man who had been hired to help prepare the grounds and set up the tents.

The first thing I noticed when we arrived at the Fair Grounds was the wood chips covering the grounds as far as I could see in every direction. "Look at that," I said, pointing to the wood chips.

"I don't see why they've put these down. It's hard to walk."

"Ida, if they didn't put these down, you'd have to stop after a minute because you'd weigh ten pounds extra per shoe from all the red clay glued to it. When it dried, this entire crowd would be stuck fast until someone came and drilled them out."

We started down the outer circle. Along both sides of the aisle were games of chance or skill, such as casting loops, shooting pellet guns, or throwing baseballs. The first ride we came to was a Loop-de-loop. This one had two, opposing, bullet-shaped seats that went over and under vertically.

When the ride was over, I realized, as we came down the ramp from the dismount platform that I was suffering from having eaten recently. The food in my stomach was still turned upside down. I looked at Ida and could see from her face that she was feeling the same way. She rubbed her stomach and moaned.

"Oy veh," said Ida. "'That's Yonkers for stomach ache."

"Let's just walk around for a bit," I said. "Unless you'd like to go home."

"No, let's walk." She squeezed her eyes shut and tightened her lips, "Oy veh."

The first booth we came to as we left this section was decorated with Tarot cards, one showing a man hanging by his heels. Also, it had orbiting planets and a picture of an upturned palm, divided into labeled sections. Lettering said, 'Madame Galaxy tells who you are and foretells who you're going to be.'

Ida's eyes lit up when she read this sign. I asked, "Interested?"

She gave a nod and rushed into the tent. I followed her in.

It turned out that Madame Galaxy wasn't even a madame. She looked to be about fifteen years old. She had olive skin and jet black hair. Her eyes were bright green and lively. She was wearing a full-length crimson satin dress, the top hidden by a vintage, khaki field jacket.

She gestured to Ida to sit down in the chair in front of a small table which was covered with stacks of pamphlets and papers, saying, "Sorry about the jacket, but I'm not used to this cold, damp weather. I got a chill."

"Are you Madame Galaxy?" Ida's tone was doubtful.

"No, you can think of me as a future Madame Galaxy. My mother, the fifth Madame Galaxy has a chill, and a fever, and is home in bed. I'll do the same reading she would give you. One-half price, one dollar instead of two. Same reading."

"How could it be the same reading?" asked Ida.

"Because we were both taught by my grandmother. Look here, I'll do a reading, and you don't pay if you don't like what you hear. Okay?"

"Sure, that's good." Ida was now beaming in happy anticipation. She seemed to have gotten over her nausea and it was a pleasure for me to see her like this. "So, I should call you Miss Galaxy?"

"Okay." The young woman spread about a dozen cards out across the middle of the table. She said to Ida, "Put your hands on the table, palm up."

She looked up at me and said, "You need to wait outside."

But I didn't leave, still curious to see what she was going to do.

Ida put her hands down, palms up. Miss Galaxy leaned forward, staring at Ida's palms, while she moved her extended right arm over the cards, with her hand hovering about six inches above them. Three times, her hand dipped like a dowsing rod, and she slid the card under her hand at the moment to her side of the table.

She sat back and looked up at Ida, saying, "You are not from here. Tell me where you're from and the date and hour of your birth."

"I was born in Yonkers, New York, on November 11th, 1918, at 5 o'clock in the afternoon."

Hearing this, I was unable to stop myself from saying. "What a strange coincidence. You were born on the day The Great War ended, and I was born the day it started."

Miss Galaxy glanced at me, "I need quiet to be able to give you a good reading."

She turned back to Ida and added, "You need to ask your friend to leave. A reading is strictly personal and confidential."

I murmured to Ida, "I'll wait out front," and left the tent.

There were stands all around serving things to eat that I hadn't had in a long time, such as corn-on-the-cob and caramel apples. I was still trying to decide whether eating would cure me or kill me, when I saw Ida leaving the tent. As I walked up to her, I saw that her nausea had returned or, at least, that's what I thought at first.

"Ida, you don't look good. Are you about to throw up?"

"No, let's just walk around some more."

After about a dozen steps, she said, "I need to leave. Are you ready to go?"

"Of course, let's go."

As we left the gate, Ida suggested we walk as far as Meredith College and take the bus from there. And that's what we did. I didn't understand what was going on with Ida. But she didn't say anything, just looked down at the ground or at the floorboards of the bus. We got of at Glenwood Avenue and stood on the corner of Glenwood and Hillsboro for a few minutes. I was waiting for Ida to get her legs under her again.

After a few minutes, Ida said, "I'd like to talk, someplace quiet and private. Not the diner. Let's go to that oyster bar on Jones Street, near where I live."

"Sure.

Once we had a corner booth and ordered bowls of chowder, Ida seemed to fade in some way. One moment she was there like always. The next she just wasn't there anymore. Her face was blank and there were tears on her cheeks. I waited, saying nothing. It was about ten minutes before the waiter brought our soup. During that time, Ida sat without moving, without speaking, her face still blank, her eyes closed.

Even with the soup on the table, Ida didn't open her eyes. Maybe ten more minutes passed in exactly the same way. Neither of us spoke nor touched our soup.

Then, Ida opened her eyes and said, "I need to talk. Will you listen? Please, don't say anything. Just listen."

"I'll do that."

Here is what she told me.

"My father beat my mother. He didn't beat me. If he got angry with me, he'd just go ahead and beat her for it. So, I had to keep shut up. I couldn't stand it when he beat her. He was arrested several times when neighbors called the police to complain about the racket. I did my part by screaming and crying. When I was fourteen, I gave up thinking that if I stayed I could fix it. One day I just left. I got a job sweeping and helping out at a beauty shop in Yonkers. When I had been there a year, Charlene, the owner, made me an apprentice operator.

"I refused to go back to the house. The only times I got to see my mother was when my father was away. She'd come to the shop. Twice she let me give her the treatments I was learning.

"Then, just after my seventeenth birthday, my father beat my mother for the last time. Somehow this was different from all the other times. She died.

I went to see her body at the morgue. She was so pitiful lying there on that slab.

"My father was arrested. After holding him for two months, they charged him with murder. That night, he took off his trousers and twisted the legs tight as a rope. He managed to hang himself from a bar of the window.

"I went to see his body at the morgue. You know, I hated him at that time. For what he'd done to both of us, but especially my mother. Now, sitting here and remembering how he looked on that slab, even though I still hate him, I can't help but think he looked just as pitiful as my mother did. This is a breakthrough for me. For years, I've been refusing to admit that I blamed her, too, for letting it happen, and I've hated her as much as I've hated him.

"I left Yonkers for good the next day. I'll never go back. Not even to visit my mother's grave. That's all over for me. Finished."

As she talked, an occasional tear ran down her cheek and fell onto the tabletop. She put her head down on the table. I couldn't tell what she was doing. She wasn't sobbing.

I wasn't sure she was right. It certainly didn't seem over to me. Where was her hard edge now, when she needed it?

§

I left the hotel in search of breakfast the next morning and found Lana waiting on the pavement in front of the hotel.

"I came by to tell you that I found Marla's grave yesterday," she said.

"I'm happy to hear that, for your sake. I have to tell you that we stopped looking after you showed up still alive. How did you find her?"

"I got the idea that if they hid her in a grave with other people, maybe they're only hiding her and not the others. So, I created a missing uncle and went down there and told the attendant that on February 14, my alcoholic uncle disappeared and asked if there was any chance he had ended up there.

"He went through a big volume on the counter and said, 'We had three unidentified bodies picked up that weekend. They were taken to the pauper's cemetery that Monday in the late afternoon.'"

"Can you say which grave?" I asked him.

"'Sure, hold on a moment,' and he looked in another book. 'That's funny,' he said. 'Four were taken over in the ambulance when we only had three to start with. There's a mistake somewhere.'"

"Do you have a grave ID?"

"'Yes,' he replied, and gave me a number."

"I went to the cemetery, bought some white roses and left them on her grave along with a short note. Then, I sent off a letter to her parents, telling them how to find her. When I get some defense money, I'm going to put up a marker."

I looked Lana in the face as she said this last and saw she was smiling through her tears, happy to have this closure with her friend.

"Wonderful, Lana, good work. You're born to it, even getting the proof that was the right grave—the fourth derelict."

"That was just lucky," she said.

"It sounds like more than luck, Lana. What got you going in the first place?"

"After Papa Mose told me what happened with Parker—do you know that story?" Lana asked.

"Not the whole thing."

"You'd never hear it from Granbelle. She looks at Papa through dark glasses and has never accepted that side of his life. He has a lot of support from people who run that side of town, people who like what he does, who like coming down to his place at night.

"The result is that somebody gets paid off, and Parker can't close the place down–which pisses him off. When he heard it was Mose Blue's daughter, he came right over to play his sick games, and not the first time Parker's done that.

"Anyway, by the time Papa got to the Morgue, he was so emotional that, when he saw the body, he just nodded and turned away. He was already upset and seeing that bashed-in head added to his shock."

"Why did Parker dump the body?" I asked.

"It was one more of his dirty tricks on Papa," said Lana.

§

Because my leave was up soon, Ida and I went out to the Blue Dove, where the same group was still playing some numbers Benny Goodman had recorded with the Hot Five, one of his smallish ensembles.

I told Ida that my orders had come through, and I had to be in San Diego on Monday, June First. I was going to rejoin my old outfit on Guadalcanal, where they were training and getting ready for another operation. I was kind of figuring it would be Bougainville, but like the good mud that I was, I was willing to wait and see.

Ida was in a better mood and seemed to be enjoying herself. I don't know why, but it seemed like the right moment to talk about our future.

"Ida, before I leave...." I didn't get a chance to finish because she interrupted me.

"I've been waiting for the right moment to tell you what Miss Galaxy said. Are you ready?"

"As I can be," I said.

"We're going to have a baby! Can you believe it?"

Her face was all aglow, and she even looked pregnant.

"So what they taught in the seventh grade was wrong," I said. "You don't have to have sex first."

"Her name is Polly," Ida continued.

"Listen, keep me informed and write every day, especially about the pregnancy."

"I'll write you every day, of course," said Ida, "but don't be silly. I'm talking about Miss Galaxy's prediction."

"If you do turn up pregnant while I'm away, I'm gonna sue for divorce," I added.

"But we're not...." Ida stopped there.

"Miss Galaxy isn't the only one who can make predictions," I said.

Speaking slowly and having to raise her voice over the band music, Ida said, "Let me understand what you're saying here. You are predicting we are going to be married. You are making an offer, over and above Miss Galaxy's prediction. Is that right?"

"Ida, you spend too much time talking business. Are you trying to negotiate a contract?"

She paused to consider an appropriate punishment, I think, for my brazen attitude.

Then, the band launched into a swing version of 'Embraceable You' and Ida started humming and singing, softly, still looking me in the eye.

Here comes the torch song torment. I recognized the symptoms and capitulated.

"Ida, once you start thinking in song lyrics, I know I'm in trouble. It could even happen that I start thinking the same way."

"What are you saying?" She said.

"Meet me tomorrow morning at 10 a.m. My train doesn't leave until tomorrow afternoon."

"But Sergeant Rollins, I have to work tomorrow. I've taken off two straight days as it is."

In a loud moonshine voice, I said, "Tell 'em the Mayor's going to marry us, and that you'll be on your honeymoon!" I'm not sure it was even a proposal, but it was the best I could do after five glasses of tax-free booze. Other people were looking to our table to see what the fuss was about.

"The Mayor's going to marry us!" Ida burbled.

"That's the idea." I leaned forward and planted a big, wet smackeroo right on her lips.

While we were kissing, a burst of applause broke out in our section of the club. The bandleader turned around and took a bow.

§

Ida and I had our honeymoon night, about which no more will be said except that we were both happy and I was for once at peace with the world.

After Ida went to sleep, I lay there thinking about going back onto active duty, wondering about the welfare of men I knew. Then, I started to wonder about LaBelle. It seemed to me that her getting her legs knocked out from under her by the return of Lana and Jerome couldn't have come at a worse time. She needed to be standing strong on those legs if she was going to succeed with Bats. It was some undertaking at any age to go from laundress to running a mansion in a single step. At her age and given how long she had been grooved into her life among the sheets, I wasn't sure it was even possible.

Then, the next I knew it was the morning of our big day. We drove in the A to her office where she needed to pass out instructions, or whatever she does there when she's taking a day off. We decided to walk to see the Mayor since we were going from there to do our honeymoon shopping, though we already had had as much of a honeymoon as we were going to get.

The route we took to see Mayor Bats was down Fayetteville Street, where all the shops were. All the way down that street, Ida was window-shopping, making out her list for later.

While she was occupied with that I got back onto the question of Labelle and, also, Lana. Would she relent and stay in Raleigh, given the depth of feeling she had awakened in LaBelle? Obviously, they could make it work, being together. She could even live there with LaBelle and the Mayor.

Sure enough, Ida was working on a list, and we had to stop several times for her to take notes in her little brown book.

We got to the mansion before the Mayor was up and about and were waiting for him when he came down from his rooms. Ida and I had already talked it over, so it was all going to be simple from our side.

But first, after some hesitation and anxiety, I asked him how LaBelle was doing in her job and how she liked living there in the mansion.

"Are you sure you really want to know?" This question from Bats really took the starch out of me.

"My boy, your worries are misplaced. It is uncanny how well she fits in," said Bats. "It's like she was born to do it. I don't know if you realize, but everyone in here reports to her except for yours truly, the Mayor. But I can see that will not last. She's going to be running the whole city before long.

"You can see for yourself. I'll take you to her quarters when we've worked out what you came for."

When we told Mayor Bats what we wanted to do, good ol' boy that he was, he could hardly contain his joy. "My good fellow, I've been frank with you before, and I will be again. It isn't often in politics that opportunities arise to perform great service and do yourself some good at the same time. When that happens, you know you're living right and the Good God is on your side.

"I want to do this at the auditorium on South Street, same as last time. I'll bring newspaper reporters. Maybe, I can even get a live radio broadcast. We'll have a great hullabaloo!"

Ida had a request about the ceremony. "We want it simple and direct, Mayor, straight to the point. Quick in and quick out, you might say."

"My dear lady, the hallmark of a good politician is going right to the heart of the matter. You can count on me."

We talked on for a bit, but Mayor Bats started getting restless to begin making his arrangements. He walked us through a door at the back of the main hall leading to the servant's quarters. We found ourselves in a corridor with the kitchen on our left and an open doorway to LaBelle's quarters on the right.

The Mayor said, "She is well-located here. Everyone must pass through this door to come into the mansion. The Mayor scooted off, and Ida and we entered LaBelle's new world.

Ida went through the doorway first and I followed, giving a tap on the open door, "Tatie, we've come by on official business."

Her rooms were more like an office suite than sleeping quarters. There was a desk to the right where she was seated, writing in an open notebook. To the left of us were several chairs and a table with a tea service and remnants of breakfast. Directly ahead was a window looking out onto the Mayor's rose garden and a cemetery across the street. Lana was sitting in the window seat and turned toward us as we entered the room.

There was an open doorway next to Lana, which I supposed was the entry to LaBelle's sleeping chamber.

Lana seemed relaxed and happy to see us. But, LaBelle was like a different person. That seriousness of intent that I had always put down as something she brought with her into the twentieth century was gone and with it the stern manner which to me felt like who she was. That was gone too, as though she had shed a weight she had always carried.

Now, on top of all that, she was looking at me with a soft and kind expression, one that revealed exactly what she was feeling at the moment. I had never seen her do that. Her face had always been calm but unemotional.

LaBelle stood up to greet us and said, "Welcome to our new life."

Ida was, as usual, a lot quicker than I was, and she said, "That's a beautiful dress, LaBelle, and I love the pearls."

LaBelle was wearing a belted, purple satin dress that came to her ankles and a single strand, pearl necklace that came to her waist. Her hair was rolled up somehow with a silk net over it. She was wearing an open housekeeper's smock over her dress.

"Tatie, the first thing you said to me when I came back from the Pacific, was that I didn't look like the same person. I'd say the same, twice over for you. I feel like asking Lana to introduce us."

Lana said, "Talking about her clothes, you should see her closet and what the Mayor has done for her. Even the kitchen staff call him 'Bats' but should call him Mister Mayor Bats. He's taken Granbelle out shopping every afternoon, and has already filled her closet.

Without guarding my words as much as I should have, I said, "He is a man of many parts and always surprising."

Lana said, "Many parts, like Lon Chaney in the motion pictures."

I turned to Ida, saying, "Ida, this is the young woman, the cause of so much heart-ache and so much joy. Lana, this is my friend Ida Patini."

They nodded to one another. I turned back to LaBelle, "Is Lana going to stay here with you?"

Before LaBelle had a chance to speak, Lana said, "I'm not staying. I'm tired of being poor. I want to get in on that National Defense money, like Rosie the Riveter."

"I was just up in Newport News with my friend Red. They turn out a new liberty ship every day at those shipyards."

"You know better than that, Holly. I could never get a job there. I'm going out west, to Hollywood. Well, near Hollywood, where they build airplanes."

LaBelle gestured toward the chairs around the tea table. But Ida shook her head. "I'm sorry, LaBelle, we've got a lot of shopping to do. The official business Holly was referring to is our marriage. We came by to invite you to a ceremony this afternoon at the auditorium. I imagine you can just come over with the Mayor who is going to marry us."

"That's wonderful, Ida. I'm so happy to hear that. Moon, let me give you both a hug."

Lana also came over and there were hugs going around. I even got to sneak in a hug for Ida.

She then turned to LaBelle and asked her, "Why do you call him Moon, LaBelle? Nobody else does."

"Well, it's a simple story from when he was small. He used to sleep over and take naps at my house. When I woke him up, if it was morning, I'd say, 'Rise and shine, Merry Sunshine'. If it was evening, I'd say, 'Rise and shine, Jolly Moon'. Jerome heard me say that one night and started calling him Moon Blue, and they pretended they were brothers when they played marbles in the front yard with Jerome's friends. We both just called him Moon most of the time after that."

Ida looked at me with one of those I-knew-it-wasn't-so looks. "He told me it was because he had a moon-pie face."

LaBelle laughed. "No, he had a thin face and beautiful blond hair that turned white in the summer sun."

Ida grabbed my hand saying, "We've got to go now. We don't have time to prepare the wedding I'd like, but I'm going to squeeze in as much as I can."

We left the mansion and went straight to the bank. Ida waited out front while I went in and picked up six-month's back pay, walking out with almost $200 in my denims.

"Okay, I've got the dough and you've got the go," I announced.

"First we're going to buy you a zoot suit with a reet pleat. Then I can wear my Satin Sadie outfit again when we go back down to Mose's place. We'll get you swimming trunks and a bathing suit for me, plus a travel outfit in dark gray."

We hurried over to Fayetteville Street to Hudson-Belks. I wasn't sure of the wisdom of buying new civvies just as I was about to go back onto active service, but Ida was not to be stopped. We spent $180 in the two hours we had before lunch. I had a new suit, not the zoot one, sports jacket with slacks, two pull-overs, and four new shirts.

When Ida came out of the dressing room in her new gray suit, her face appeared to me to have a rose halo tinted with gold, and even her suit was shimmering.

We went to lunch, wearing our new clothes, at our favorite place, the cafeteria at Hudson-Belk. It was self-serve, and there were waiters, well turned out, ready to bring more of what you had, or wine, or coffee.

Soon, we were in place and eating, and this was my chance to clear up a few details, "I didn't know what you meant by a zoot suit with a reet pleat."

"I'm surprised, since you were talking about Cab Calloway the other day."

"Okay, he sometimes wears a long jacket with watch chain and baggy pants."

"The pants aren't baggy. They're very high-waisted, wide at the knees and narrow at the ankles."

"How come you know so much about it, Ida?"

"Don't forget I'm from Yonkers, not far from the Cotton Club, where he works."

"You got your Satin Sadie routine from there?"

"No, I've known one or two Satin Sadies. I may have exaggerated a little."

Never having been up north, I couldn't form a picture of Yonkers. But I was closing in on something that bothered me the night we went to Mose's barroom to see Leroy.

"If I went to Mose's place in a Cab Calloway costume like you went as Satin Sadie, I'd feel like I came from a minstrel show wearing blackface."

"That's like telling me you can be LaBelle's champion, but you can't dress like she does. That sounds like segregation talk to me."

"I don't follow, Ida. You want me to wear a pettiskirt and shimishirt?"

"Cute idea. No, you say that it's a black man's suit if Cab Callaway wears it. What about the suit Franklin Roosevelt wears? Is that a white man's suit? No, you don't describe his suit that way. But, in fact, a suit is just a suit."

I was struck by how Ida's remark reminded me of my recent talk with LaBelle. Ida was waiting patiently for me to say something. I told her about that talk with LaBelle and finished up with the story about the last time I saw Sergeant Tipper and how angry he got over what I said about segregation.

Without hesitation, Ida boiled it down for me. "How is it going to work out to force segregation talk into your relationship with LaBelle? A relationship that began before you caught the bug yourself."

197

"Everyone who grows up here catches the segregation bug. I know that."

"Fine, I bet you do. But you sound like a hypocrite to her because she sees you have the bug while putting your foot down about segregation."

"Damn, Ida. I think you got something there. You mean that when I talk to her about all that segregation business, it just makes her see me as a segregationist. Is that it?"

Ida pursed her lips in thought before answering, then said, "Yes, that may be what it comes down to. You're a hypocrite because you're a segregationist condemning segregation."

"How about Sergeant Tipper?" I asked.

"I would guess he would think about it the same way she did." She gave me a big hug and added, "I love you in these clothes. I wish you didn't have to put that uniform on ever again."

§

The ceremony was held in the public auditorium, opened to the public at the Mayor's request. The Hall was three-quarters full, with reporters churning around, photographers' flashbulbs like beacons flashing in the dim room, and the Mayor intoning into several radio microphones.

True to His Honor's word, he went through the ceremony as quick as he had once ducked a bat.

"We're here to join these two in matrimony unless somebody objects. No? Let's do it. Ida, you want to marry Holly?"

"I do."

"Holly, you want to marry Ida?"

"I do."

"Okay, you're hitched."

Ida said, "Just a moment, Mister Mayor. I want to hear the correct words, the declaration, or maybe I should say the correct designation."

"Designation?" said the Mayor.

"Yes," said Ida, "the proper designation."

"Ida, do you mean I pronounce you etcetera?"

"I do."

198

"All right. I now pronounce you…" the Mayor came to a full stop. He mumbled, all the while staring at Ida, "proper designation, proper designation."

"Ladies and Gentlemen, Ida has requested that I use the proper designation in declaring their marriage. Therefore," he turned back toward Ida and me and gestured for us to rejoin hands.

"Ida and Holly, I now pronounce you woman and husband." The Mayor intoned, then looked at Ida and said, "How was that, Ida?"

Ida laughed and said, "Mayor Bats, I couldn't have put it better myself."

Reverting to that earlier voice, the Mayor said, "In that case, Mrs. Rollins, you may kiss the husband."

After we had kissed, the Mayor took each of us by the elbow and said, facing the guests, "Let me be the first to introduce you to the new married couple, Misses and Mister Ida Rollins."

There has been some dispute over what happened next, but I know for sure that when His Honor uttered those words, Ida's girls, her operators, started with shrieks of laughter and continued to shriek for the entire rest of the celebration.

As Ida and I walked down from the stage where we had been standing with the Mayor, I said to him over my shoulder, "Thanks, Mayor, she'll never forget you for this. Me, neither."

We found out that what he omitted from the ceremony, he made up for in the celebration of it. There were half a dozen photographers making sure everybody was documented with an official photograph to be mounted in leather-bound albums that were among the presents for the bride. The wedding cake was served with champagne on ice. The Mayor had ordered cases of champagne and large blocks of ice. Two long tables were loaded with gifts for the bride and groom. The bridesmaids, including all of Ida's operators and friends, were each given expensive luggage filled to overflowing with lotions and perfumes.

Afterwards, we stood to receive the congratulations of friends and relations. It was good preparation for my return to duty. After half-an-hour of photographs and greetings, I felt like I was already back in combat.

I saw Mickey across the room and went over to her. She had left the Purified Parlor, and we seemed to have lost contact with her in recent days. But when I greeted her, she was all smiles and congratulations.

I asked her, "What are you doing? I haven't seen you."

Mickey looked me over and laughed. "You, of all people, should appreciate what I'm doing right now."

"How so?"

"You remember the pool sessions we had at Dad's place just before all hell broke out?"

"Don't ask me that."

"Okay, I see you do remember." Mickey was amused by whatever it was she was going to tell me. "I've got a sucker list of about a dozen men. I take twenty bucks a week each. You know, Buck was right when he teased you about being hooked by the way I shoot pool. It drives men crazy, just like it used to drive you crazy. I could probably take them for fifty dollars a week if I wanted to be greedy."

"You're right, Mickey. That's rich."

"I've found out I'm ambitious when it comes to the sporting life. Who'd have guessed it? I been giving Mosconi a look. I don't know. I can't beat him right now. But it's not impossible."

"I'm happy for you, Mickey. I was afraid you might be sad about the way everything turned out."

"I regret that it wrecked what Chester and I had together."

"I've heard that when all else fails, try prayer."

"I don't know how to pray."

"Just repeat after me. Ready?"

"Ok."

"Good Lord,"

"Good Lord,"

"Please, ask an angel to bring Chester back to me."

"Please, ask an angel to bring Chester back to me."

"Thank you."

"Thank you."

I gave Mickey a big hug and said to her, "I believe that covers it, Mickey."

Mickey went out onto the terrace.

I noticed that LaBelle and Ida were coming for me, with Lana just behind them.

Ida said, "We have to leave in just a few minutes, if we're going to get you to the station on time."

"Mister and Misses Moon, congratulations and every happiness."

"Congratulations to you, LaBelle, on your success in your new job." I was happy but not surprised it had turned out so well.

LaBelle couldn't come to the station because she was working. So, I said my goodbye to her at the door of the Hall. "I'm happy to see you dressed as you are and the light of Bats' world."

LaBelle Blue smiled and shifted her position in order to speak to both Ida and myself. "You didn't manage to break down that fence," she said. "But, somehow, the war has made you come out from behind your own. I'm proud of the way you care about other people. I'm sure you'll come back from this war, have children, continue to grow and love your neighbor as yourself."

I kissed LaBelle on both cheeks in the French way, and she did the same to me.

"Tatie," I said, "thank you for being patient and understanding with me. If I seem like a hypocrite to you, then I guess I am a hypocrite, but I came by it honestly."

Turning to Ida, I said, "Did that make any sense?"

Ida looked at LaBelle who was looking at me like she did when I was five years old with nails through my hand. Ida turned back to me and said, "No, but I think LaBelle will give you the chance to keep working on it. You don't have to get it right in this moment."

I was still holding LaBelle's hand and we each gave a last squeeze. I turned to Lana and told her I wished her well in her trip out west.

Lana said, "Thanks to you and the Mayor. I wouldn't have been able to go if Granbelle was not so well fixed. With that taken care of, I should be able to spend a couple of years out there and come back here ready to settle down."

Both Ida and I gave her a last hug and turned away to head for the exit.

Standing in front of us was a man I had seen before, with black hair, a five o'clock shadow, husky, not tall. But there was about him a kind of friendly look directed toward Ida and myself.

"Congratulations, my friend," he said to me. To Ida, he said, "My name is Chester Carmichael, Buck's friend and ex-employer."

I looked at this man with surprise, while at the same time being happy to see him.

"How did you get here," I asked him.

"Sonny drove me in my old Packard."

"Hard to think of Sonny as an angel."

There was a puzzled expression on Chester's face as he said, "I don't understand."

"Never mind," I said.

Ida found her voice to ask, "What do you mean, Buck's friend? Don't you mean to say Buck's would-be assassin? Didn't you send men to kill him?

"No, there were two men after him. But I didn't send them."

Ida said, "These men are hoodlums. They tried to force people to give them information."

"Chester," I needed to check on a loose end. "How do Sonny and Anders feel about Mickey? They know she didn't go back on their deal, right?"

"There could have been a problem, if Buck hadn't have ended up dead. They're satisfied with that result. No worries." Chester spoke these words with such conviction that I knew that he was a guarantor of that arrangement, who knows how.

Chester seemed to hesitate, like he wanted to say more, but he didn't add anything.

I stared at Chester who shifted his weight back and forth a few times.

Ida said, "Explain it all to Mickey. She's the one who's been left alone."

I said to him, "Mickey's on the terrace. If you propose to her and if she accepts, then just tell the Mayor to marry you as a last favor he can do for me. Believe me, it won't take long."

Ida and I went over to the door and stood there, thanking people who were leaving. I grabbed her hand and said, "Let's go on over to the station. I've got to find Red to get the car keys."

We walked out onto the front porch of the auditorium. LaBelle and Mose came out right behind us.

The four of us found ourselves looking down at a man standing at the bottom of the steps looking up at us. I swear to you that my hair stood straight up in dread and wonder. Here on these steps was a sailor I thought was sleeping with the fish, next to Cap. Big as life, standing there looking at me with mild, friendly expectations as though I had just sent him out to buy a pack of cigarettes, and he was ready to hand them over along with my change, was Buck Rains.

Gaping at him, unable to speak, I heard Mose, who didn't know Buck was dead or supposed to be dead, lash out with, "Mister Buck Rogers, how ya doin'?"

"Happy to be ashore, Mister Mose."

Buck started up the stairs just as Chester and Mickey came through the door and stopped behind LaBelle. Buck seemed to drag his feet taking the next few steps, but he came on until he was standing in front of LaBelle, looking past her to Chester.

"I ain't running from you again."

My brain felt as squeezed and dried-out as yesterday's breakfast orange. Or, maybe, it was just two steps behind in the conversation. Things were happening too fast for me to adjust to them. Buck's alive? How did Mose get to know him? Why did Mose call him 'Mister Buck Rogers'?

After about three ticks, Chester said, "I don't know why you ever ran from me, Buck. I've thought of you as a friend gone astray, one in danger, but not from me."

"You murdered my father."

"Buck, I swear to you that I wasn't a part of that. I know it looks bad because I was in Asheville at the time, putting pressure on you."

I was still watching Buck as closely as a snake charmer watches his snake.

Lana came out onto the porch with Jerome. Her appearance caught Buck's eye. He turned his head a moment away from Chester.

The latter reacted by looking over his shoulder to see who had come up behind him. Mickey, also, turned to see who it was.

Looking back at Chester, Buck continued, "You're a liar. It was the blood feud."

I shifted around to get a better view of Lana, who reacted to my movement and waved her hand at me behind LaBelle's back.

Then, Red came out onto the porch, stopping behind Lana. I watched as he looked around until he saw Buck. Earlier, at Lana's place, I saw his superstitious streak. It was easy to imagine his heart skipping beats and his skin crawling up his spine.

While I was watching Red, my brain started to catch up, to the point of getting ready to ask Mose why he said what he did. But he beat me to it.

Like a man struck drunk, Mose started toward Buck, moving slowly while saying, "Marla called you that name, Buck Rogers."

We'll never know what might have happened, cause Buck turned, went down the steps and started across the lawn toward South Street.

Red pushed past Lana and, speaking to Mose, said, "Where, in the name of hell and damnation did Buck come from?"

Ignoring Red's outburst, Mose asked Lana, "Was it him?"

She answered, "I can't say he killed Marla. He was the secret one she was seeing."

Lana turned to me and said, "Sorry, but I'm not an expert, and it's easy to get confused between Flash Gordon and Buck Rogers."

Before Mose got a chance to respond to this news, I came out of my foxhole. My brain not only got caught up, it finally put a couple of facts together and found some connections.

"Red, remember the tabbynappers? Why did Mickey tell them how to find Buck? That never made any sense to me."

Red caught on quicker than I did, "As a loyal sister she knew his dirty secrets."

I looked over at Mickey, standing next to Chester, "Why did you tell them?"

Mickey looked from me to Chester and back again. "I guess you know why. I thought what happened to Marla was awful, but Buck told me he did it in a fit of rage that would never happen again.

You told me he killed Doll Baby and told me the horrible way that poor Leroy died. I knew the truth, you see, and that meant it was partly my fault. I couldn't just let it go on."

Chester put his arm around Mickey's shoulders and said to her, "You couldn't have known he would do these things. Turning toward me, he said, "The three of us have been together since grade school. I've never seen Buck in a rage before."

"Maybe, this is your chance to get after him," Ida said to Chester.

Chester shrugged and said, "It's a waste of my time to say I'm not after Buck. In case you've forgotten though, Anders and Sonny are sitting in my Packard behind the auditorium."

"They want blood for blood." I had finally had enough of the Blue Ridge Mountain Boys. I didn't give a damn about the blood they were avenging. What about Marla? How about Cotton or Leroy?

"I'm going after him myself."

"Not without me," said Red.

"Me too. He's caused me more misery than he has anybody else," said Mose, the giant.

Maybe Buck saw how Goliath looked to David when he lit out.

"Where did you put the car?" I asked Red who had come down in the Model-A.

He answered, "I'll show you."

"Mose, I'll pick you up right out there on South Street," I said, nodding in the direction Buck had taken.

I told Ida, "Be right back."

We ran down the steps and around the corner of the building to the parking lot, got into the car, and pulled down the back window to be able to talk to Mose when he was in the rumble seat.

I drove around front and stopped beside Mose who stepped up onto the rear bumper, lifting the front wheels off the road. Then, he settled into the rumble seat and we took off down South Street. I didn't hurry, and we checked each side street to make sure Buck hadn't turned off.

Mose saw Buck, dead ahead, and started pounding on the roof and yelling, "Hiya, hiya, giddon there, mule."

When I looked ahead, I saw him. The vicious murders of Marla and Cotton counted for a lot, certainly, but letting Leroy suffer knowing the grim death coming his way for something he didn't do was far worse.

Mose pounded on the roof again, shouting, 'Hurry up'.

I realized that in another minute we would come up to Mose's store on South Street, where Buck got to know Marla, where Leroy took the fall for him, and where I got stabbed.

LaBelle had chosen me to make him pay. She had said, "You are the one I need to find Lana's body and to find her killer." Well, here he was soon to be in our hands. Maybe it would be more accurate to say he would soon be in Mose's hands.

I said to Red, "Maybe the mountain boys have the right answer. Buck has to pay with his blood."

"Don't worry! He'll pay. Blood must be paid."

His words hit me hard. For a minute I couldn't place it. Then, I remembered that it was from my nightmare. "Why did you say that, 'Blood must be paid.'"

Red answered, "I didn't say it. You did."

I let my foot off the pedal, and the car drifted to a stop in the middle of the road, right next to the store.

Yes, that was it. I was the lay-away expert with ice in my veins, the man who had buried hundreds of marines and filled mass graves with thousands of dead Japanese soldiers.

A newsreel started in my head. After burying Powell, I was on a bulldozer filling a mass grave when I noticed a Jap still alive. He rolled over trying to drag himself out of my path. With my heart overflowing with hatred, I veered the bulldozer in his direction. He was still trying to drag himself away when I ran over him with the right-hand tread. I looked down at his bloated face with blood still gushing from his nose and mouth. Blood must be paid in blood. I hated him for Powell's death.

The newsreel changed to my four uncles lowering a wooden box into black water. But this time, I saw my father was at the foot of my mother's grave sobbing and making no effort to cover his face or disguise his wild grief.

All my life I had been over and over my memories of my mother and that grave. This was the first time I realized that it wasn't just about me. What had my father gone through, losing his wife and finding himself with my sister and myself—two young children to take care of on his own—from then until forever?

I felt Red tugging at my shirt sleeve. "Holly, are you having one of those attacks? What's going on?"

"I'm okay."

I pulled back onto South Street and continued after Buck, who was just one block ahead.

"It was the war. I was reliving an experience from the war. The Doctor told me that if I had any intense emotions, that might cause me to have flashbacks to the war."

"What kind of flashbacks are you talking about?"

"Let me tell you, a friend to Powell, that I didn't report his grave to the registration people. I left him to rot forever in a stinking swamp hole."

Before, I had felt a kind of horror over this neglect, but now I felt only grief.

"Maybe when I go back to Guadalcanal I can find him again. Where I buried him. If I can, then I could get him dug up and brought home."

"Sergeant Rollins, you gotta help me out here." Red said. "We have to go on with what we're doing. We're right on top of Buck now."

I looked ahead for Buck and saw him staring back at the Model-A. I can't imagine how we appeared to him. As we slowed down, coming up behind him, Mose was getting ready to go after him and had gotten to his feet in the rumble seat. He was leaning over the car gripping the roof on both sides with his huge fists. To Buck it may have looked as though Mose was ready to leap onto his back like Yakima Canutt, the movie stuntman, leaping off a stagecoach onto a horse.

I came up to Buck and stayed beside him as he continued to walk along.

"Get in," I told him.

"To go where and do what?" Buck demanded.

"You got a lot to pay for, my friend."

"You here to collect on it, War Hero?"

"Buck, why did you do it?"

Buck put his head down and ran a few steps, then slowed down; he couldn't outrun the A. I came up beside him again.

"Why did you kill Marla, Buck?"

"She kept threatening to make a phone call to Chester, to tell him where I was. She knew him from before the war. He used to come to South Street."

"Okay, come back with me, Buck. I don't think they're going to change the verdict of Leroy's trial. If you're lucky, who knows, they might not charge you at all."

"Go to hell, Holly. I'll never come with you."

As we were talking, Mose was climbing down from the rumble seat and getting himself ready to jump off the car, now barely moving. He was standing on the running board, close enough to reach out and touch Buck.

Red was watching Mose. He turned toward Buck and asked him, "How did you get off the ship. In Newport, I mean."

"That was easy. You're a couple of fools if you think I was crazy enough to get on that ship. As I was going up the gangplank, I saw you leave. I turned around and went into Newport News."

Buck looked up then and saw Mose. He took off running. Mose jumped down and took off right behind him. I could see it was not going to take long for Buck to leave Mose behind.

I stopped the car and turned off the engine to give myself the quiet to think about what was happening.

The hatred I felt toward Buck was being replaced by a kind of dumb sympathy. I wanted to see him pay for what he did to Leroy. At the same time, I didn't personally want to do it. Hadn't I already done more than my share? I got Leroy killed over Lana's death and, guess what, not only was he not her murderer, she wasn't even dead.

Red opened the passenger door and got out. He stooped over to look me in the face and said, "You lettin' him get away? Mose can't catch him."

"Go after him, Red. You can catch him, easy."

"Why did you stop? Are you coming apart again, Sergeant Rollins?"

"No. But my war demon must have decided to give me a break on my wedding day. I'm not going to kill anybody today. I'm going to sit here and enjoy being happy."

Red turned and took off after Buck. I could see he could still run like nobody else.

But I couldn't see how this was going to turn out. I couldn't imagine that either Mose or Red were going to kill Buck. Mose might mangle him up a bit, and Red would certainly punch him a few times. Kill him? I didn't think so.

I saw Mose stop, bending over with his hands on his knees. I hoped he had given up. I didn't want to see him keel over and lay another death to Buck Rains.

That's when I heard the Packard coming, purring like a hungry wildcat. It passed me by, sleek and powerful, sure of its prey, with Sonny and Anders in the front seat. The car went past Red and Mose, and I watched it pull up beside Buck. Moments later, it pulled away with Buck inside, swallowed up by the beast.

In that moment, I was relieved that I had not taken Buck's life. I was just managing to hold at bay the hidden grief and guilt I already had. I didn't need any more. True, I couldn't understand Mohat's teaching that LaBelle talked about, but I could understand that if you don't do it, you don't feel guilty over it. Maybe I could also understand that you don't add to the sum total of hatred in the world.

Mose and Red came back to the car, and in a few minutes we were back at the wedding reception. Our good Mayor Stinkypee had joined the crowd and was speaking with Parker Reddy.

I walked up to Parker, reached into my pocket and handed him the box holding the Medal of Honor.

"I'm certain Powell would be happy for you to have this. I've felt guilty about having it when Powell, as you point out, lost his life saving mine. I lied to you about how he died. I was angry and trying to get even with you. Powell died without ever regaining consciousness. He died quietly. In the conditions that night, there was nothing anyone could have done for him. Please don't say anything about this now. We'll have a long talk about it after the war. I'm going to write a letter to Washington and tell them what I've done with the Medal and suggest they review the events of that night and award the Medal to your brother."

Parker accepted the box with an air of justice at last done. I could agree with that entirely. That medal had been burning a hole in my pocket for too long.

"Thank you and good luck on all your future campaigns, Mister Mayor Bats. Goodbye to all of you and thanks for coming."

Ida and I hurried off to the train station.

§

On the way to camp, I woke up to the fact that the Medal of Honor had jinxed me. It had put a spell on me that, somehow, everything was my fault. I was to blame for Powell getting killed, even for how he was buried. I was to blame for getting a medal that should have gone to him. I was to blame for the whole damn war.

I thank God Almighty and Dugout Doug MacArthur, who won his Medal of Honor sitting in the back of a PT Boat that never came in contact with the enemy, that they are calling the shots and not me. I thank, also, all other officers under Doug's command that the war does not come under my authority. I'm not to blame for its chaos and destruction. I'm just a little guy who is barely able to handle his own affairs, a little guy who prefers that his friends not be blown up in his face.

Powell, rest in peace. I hope you're happy I gave the Medal to your brother. If not, I hope you got a good laugh at my expense. Goodbye and God bless you.

Wherever I was going to be sent and whatever horrors awaited me there, were not here right now. I was going to get a good night's sleep tonight. I was sure of it.

As the bus passed through the gate onto the base, I suddenly felt a great love for my comrades. I was happy to be seeing them again. I was eager and anxious to know who had survived since I had been gone. The Combat Engineers were my extended family now and for the duration.

Hopefully, back on active service I'd be able to relax when not in combat. In a war zone, you know where you stand. Yes, they are out to kill you, and the certainty of that is comforting.

One thing I forgot to mention, about what happened when I presented my marriage plan to Ida at the *Blue Dove* and told her the Mayor was going to marry us.

She said, "Oh! I have only one improvement to make to your plan!"

Of course, she would have an improvement.

In the next moment, she revealed something she had been too angry to reveal before. Her eyes filled with love as she suggested, "Let's have our honeymoon tonight. Tomorrow, there won't be time."

§

On New Georgia, in the mess-tent, we watched a moving film about the war in Great Britain which featured a song by Vera Lynn, with the lyrics:

We'll meet again, don't know where, don't know when,
But I know we'll meet again, some sunny day.

I look forward to the sunny day when I'll meet Ida again and every day kiss a photograph she sent me. It was taken of Ida wearing her mother's wedding dress that she had re-fit to herself. It was one-piece, white satin, full-length. She wore it with a pale green cap that looked like a bathing cap and a pink veil. Her dark green, wide belt had pink sequins matching the color of her veil. She was wearing bright red satin slippers.

She explained in her letter that she put forth all this effort in order to have a picture of herself in a wedding dress. I believe she is still trying to fill in the pieces to the puzzle of her ideal marriage ceremony.

Ida is smart, no question about that, but I wonder sometimes about what it's like where she comes from in Yonkers. I also wonder if she might be color-blind.

Some months later on Bougainville, I got the following news, not scuttlebutt, the real thing: Ida Patini Rollins had given birth to a daughter named Polly Patini Rollins.

Finally, I got around to saying my prayer of gratitude.

"Thank you, Miss Galaxy," I said. "We certainly got our dollar's worth."

www.ingramcontent.com/pod-product-compliance
Lightning Source LLC
Chambersburg PA
CBHW060038030426

42334CB00019B/2380